FREE THE BEAGLE

A Journey to Destinae

Other books by Roy H. Williams:

The Wizard of Ads
Turning Words into Magic and Dreamers into Millionaires

Secret Formulas of the Wizard of Ads

Magical Worlds of the Wizard of Ads
Tools and Techniques for Profitable Persuasion

Accidental Magic
The Wizard's Techniques for Writing Words Worth 1,000 Pictures

FREE THE BEAGLE

A Journey to Destinae

Roy H. Williams

Bard Press
Austin • Atlanta

FREE THE BEAGLE
A Journey to Destinae

Printed in the United States of America.

Permission to reproduce or transmit in any form or by any means, electronic or mechanical, including photocopying and recording, or by an information storage and retrieval system, must be obtained by writing to the publisher at the address below:

Bard Press
An imprint of Longstreet Press
2974 Hardman Court
Atlanta, Georgia 30305
404-254-0110
www.bardpress.com

This is a work of fiction. All the characters and events portrayed herein are either fictitious or are used fictitiously.

Excerpts from Neil Simon's *The Odd Couple* reprinted by permission of the author.

Ordering Information

To order additional copies, contact your local bookstore or call 800-945-3132. Quantity discounts are available.
ISBN 1-885167-57-1 paperback

Library of Congress Cataloging-in-Publication Data
Williams, Roy H.
   Free the beagle : a journey to Destinae / Roy H. Williams.
      p.   cm.
      ISBN 1-885167-57-1
      1. Conduct of life. I. Title.
BJ1597 .W55 2002
158.1--dc21

                                    2002074431

The author may be contacted at the following address:
Roy H. Williams
Wizard Academy
1760 FM 967
Buda, TX 78610
512-295-5700 voice, 512-295-5701 fax
www.WizardAcademy.com

Credits

Developmental Editor: Pennie Williams
Editor: Jeff Morris
Proofreading: Deborah Costenbader
Cover design: Hespenheide Design
Illustration: Mathew Reynolds
Text design/art direction/production: Jeff Morris

First printing: July 2002

To Rex, on the occasion of his 21st birthday.

May your beagle never be tethered.

FREE THE BEAGLE
A Journey to Destinae

CONTENTS

"I have always been a quarter of an hour before my time, and it has made a man of me."

– LORD NELSON

"Unfaithfulness in the keeping of an appointment is an act of clear dishonesty. You may as well borrow a person's money as his time."

– HORACE MANN

"I give it as my deliberate and solemn conviction that the individual who is habitually tardy in meeting an appointment, will never be respectful or successful in life."

– REV. FRANKLIN W. FISK

"If there is one German custom you should learn and stick to, it is punctuality. An invitation for 4 PM means EXACTLY 4 PM. Not 15 minutes earlier and not 10 minutes later. Fashionably late is not a German custom. Germans, particularly business professionals, are sticklers about being on time."

– MATTHIAS AUTRATA

"Twenty-three and a quarter minutes past," Uncle Matthew was saying furiously, "in precisely six and three-quarter minutes the darned fellow will be late."

– NANCY MITFORD

"Time like an ever rolling stream bears all its sons away."

– H. G. WELLS, *MIND AT THE END OF ITS TETHER*

"One can think of ordinary, real, time as a horizontal line. On the left, one has the past, and on the right, the future. But there's another kind of time in the vertical direction. This is called imaginary time, because it is not the kind of time we normally experience. But in a sense, it is just as real as what we call real time."

– PROF. STEPHEN HAWKING, FROM A PUBLIC LECTURE,
"THE BEGINNING OF TIME"

Destinae (des • tin • AY): A city
that exists in vertical time. The
destination of every Traveler.

1
Town Square

The lawyer ran down the checklist in his mind as rapidly as his feet marched down the sidewalk. He saw the shoeshine chair, the clock, the newspaper stand; the courthouse was just ahead. Papers. He could feel his briefcase jangling at the end of his arm, but had he remembered to place the documents inside? He stopped succinctly, spread his kerchief smoothly across the top of the newspaper stand, and lowered his black leather case upon it. He dialed the combination. Click-click. Yes,

correctly bound and properly stored. Shoes polished? He looked down; his own stern reflection glared back at him from twin black mirrors. He wasn't unfriendly, whatever people might say; no, he was dignified. And busy, very busy. It was just too bad people couldn't tell the difference. He felt the familiar cold bulge ticking beneath his left vest pocket. Tick-tick-tick-tick-tick-tick-tick. But was it accurately set? A gold chain dragged the helpless timepiece from its place of slumber and a discriminating eye compared its jerking second hand to that of the official clock in the exact center of Town Square. Precision! Satisfied, he returned the watch to its proper place, its crystal face turned inward for protection. He looked up to admire the courthouse and ran his tongue smoothly across his teeth. But what was this? The headline stared across the counter at him: "King's Son to Be Tested."

How the kingdom had buzzed when the King's son had been found! But no time to think of that now. He folded his crisp kerchief into six starched squares and placed it directly over his heart.

A place for everything and everything in its place.

Plan your work and work your plan.

Good enough never is.

The human brain is divided into two main sections, called "hemispheres," which contain complementary abilities referred to as "left-brain" and "right-brain." When and how you prefer to access the abilities of these hemispheres determines much of your personality and behavior.

Logic and "correctness" are the province of the left hemisphere; intuition and creativity are regarded as right-hemisphere skills. Because left-brain skills are more easily evaluated, schools tend to favor left-brain modes of thinking while downplaying the right-brain ones. Left-brain scholastic subjects focus on logical thinking, analysis, and accuracy. Right-brain subjects focus on aesthetics, feeling, and creativity.

Left Brain	Right Brain
Intellectual	Intuitive
Objective	Subjective
Analyze	Synthesize
Facts	Concepts
Deconstruct	Connect the dots
Detail focused	Big picture
Judgment	Perception
Perfecting	Accepting
Yang	Yin
Language skills	Musical appreciation

2
The Courthouse

The lawyer loved the courthouse. No matter how warm the day, the courthouse was always cold. Its polished marble and unyielding granite stood in hard contrast to the fuzzy world outside. Silent as a tomb, its hallways echoed the click of clocks and the fall of feet, but never the human heart.

The lawyer scanned the docket in the courthouse lobby, expecting to see his case assigned to the court of Judge Logic, whose calculated machinations made his decisions perfectly predictable. Judge Logic was always dressed in perfect black and white.

Judge Grey was another matter.

Oh, no. The lawyer was to appear before Judge Grey today. And the scheduled time was now. Right now.

Stepping briskly into the courtroom, the lawyer heard Judge Grey call his name before the bailiff had even announced his arrival. "Counselor Intellect," boomed the judge, "this beagle must go to the city of Destinae! And you are to go with it!"

Destinae! What a wonderful . . . ! Beagle? Did the judge say "beagle"? Surely the word had been "legal."

To the judge's right, a small sound came from beneath the bailiff's station. Good God, it was a dog! Resting here in the courtroom, its smelly head yawning above its filthy paws! The lawyer glared in sharp disdain. He imagined that he could smell dog breath from across the room.

"Counselor Intellect, are you listening?"

Turning his now steely gaze toward the judge, the lawyer replied, "Yes, Your Honor, I'm listening. Your instructions were that I should take this beagle to Destinae. Now, if we may adjourn until tomorrow, I will calculate our projected departure date based upon the assumption of a speedy resolution of all outstanding obligations."

"You are to depart at sundown."

"I will most certainly plan for a sunset departure on the day of our leaving, Your Honor, should that remain your instruction, but I would remind Your Honor that a morning departure offers many advantages to journeying travelers."

"You are to depart at sundown *today*, Counselor Intellect."

"Today?" replied the lawyer.

In a sweeping motion, the judge lifted his watch with his left hand and raised his gavel with his right. Glancing at his watch, he said, "You have eight hours to make yourself ready for Destinae." BANG went the gavel. The judge leaped to his feet. The bailiff shouted "All rise!" and the courtroom noisily obeyed.

"But-but-but-" stammered the lawyer.

Peering over the rims of his glasses, the towering judge said, "You have questions, Counselor Intellect?"

"What about my cases?"

As he strode toward the exit behind his bench, Judge Grey answered over his shoulder: "They have all been reassigned."

"Surely there is a schedule — charts, maps, a budget?"

Framed now in the doorway to his private chambers, Judge Grey turned to face the lawyer. "Your journey will take what it takes."

And he was gone.

Staring into the distance, the lawyer stood silent before the judge's bench as the gallery shuffled toward the exits.

Surely an enemy has done this to me, but who?

Who?

Who?

"Aim at perfection in everything, though in most cases it is unattainable. However, they who aim at it, and persevere, will come much nearer to it than those whose laziness and despondency make them give it up as unattainable."

– LORD CHESTERFIELD

"If you expect perfection from people, your whole life is a series of disappointments, grumblings and complaints. If, on the contrary, you pitch your expectations low, taking folks as the inefficient creatures which they are, you are frequently surprised by having them perform better than you had hoped."

– BRUCE BARTON

FELIX: I can't help myself. I drive everyone crazy. A marriage counselor once kicked me out of his office. He wrote on my chart, Lunatic! . . . I don't blame her. It's impossible to be married to me.

OSCAR: It takes two to make a rotten marriage. (Lies back down on the couch.)

FELIX: You don't know what I was like at home. I bought her a book and made her write down every penny we spent. Thirty-eight cents for cigarettes, ten cents for a paper. Everything had to go in the book. And then we had a big fight because I said she forgot to write down how much the book was. . . . Who could live with anyone like that?

OSCAR: An accountant! . . . What do I know? We're not perfect. We all have faults.

FELIX: Faults? We have a maid who comes in to clean three times a week. And on the other days, Frances does the cleaning. And at night, after they've both cleaned up, I go in and clean the whole place again. I can't help it. I like things clean. Blame it on my mother. I was toilet trained at five months old.

– THE ODD COUPLE, NEIL SIMON, 1965

3
Poindexter

How long he had stood stone-statue, the lawyer did not know. But when he regained his sense of time and place, the only sound he could hear was the silence of cavernous emptiness. Funny how it could echo. And the only sensation he could feel was of a slight weight upon the tops of his feet.

The beagle.

As the lawyer turned his gaze reluctantly downward, the dog's natural perfume wafted up and tweaked his nose. Seeing that the lawyer had finally regained his senses, the beagle leaped joyfully, wiggling and skittering and thrashing the room with her tail. But the lawyer saw none of this; he was standing once again like stone — mortified and transfixed by the sight of dog slobber on his shiny black shoes.

At that instant, Poindexter, the courthouse cat, strolled past the open door. In a blink, the beagle flew out the door, across the lobby, and into the town square beyond. Arooo! Aroo-aroo! Remembering his duty and obligation, the lawyer marched angrily after her.

Oh, what an untidy sight confronted the lawyer as he stepped beneath the sky! Poindexter was a blurry, furry ball bouncing between the shoeshine chair and the newspaper stand with the beagle right behind him. Newspapers, shoe brushes, and tins of polish were scattered about the lawn. Aroo! Aroo-aroo! Feet scrambling for purchase, the beagle tried to climb the side of the stand. Poindexter, convinced that the dog would succeed, dove in a valiant display of feline grace to the base of the official clock and, before you could say "Holly Golightly," was perched at the very top of it.

Striding purposefully to the center of the melee, the lawyer yanked at the beagle's leather collar and felt the touch of cold metal beneath his palm. He lifted the poor dog up by it and read the name on the finely engraved tag: "Intuition," he said aloud. "So the animal has a name. But what are these words in fine print beneath it?" The lawyer lifted the collar and the choking beagle a little closer to his eyes so that he might make out the tiny words in the dimming light of afternoon.

The world stood still.

The lawyer lowered the collar and the beagle gently to the ground. Quickly he removed his belt and, slipping its tip beneath the dog's collar, looped it back through the buckle to form a makeshift leash. Then, without another word, he walked away with the beagle in tow. The only sound the lawyer could hear was the thunder of the tag's eight tiny words in his mind: "A Gift for the Son of the King."

Poindexter was nowhere in sight.

23

4
The Library

The library had been a terrible disappointment. Not only were there no maps to the royal city of Destinae, but his research had yielded far more questions than answers. In all of his reading, he could find no account of any traveler ever returning from a trip there. Even worse, he could find no agreement among the writers who wrote of their journeys. One writer told of laboriously hacking his way through a jungle wilderness; another wrote of sailing uncharted seas. And if this alone were not confusing enough, yet another told stories of glittering parties and celebrities met along the way.

Would the lawyer need a machete, a boat, or a tuxedo?

The one thing that all the writers seemed to agree upon was the vital importance of following Polaris. But who was this Polaris, and where was he to be found?

How unfair! All of this was wrong, wrong, wrong. Who could expect him to complete his assignment when he had not been given clear instructions? Where was the list of steps to follow? Why were there no guidelines, no policies, no rules? Only a fool would demand that he undertake such a journey. Only a fool would insist that he begin at sunset. Only a fool would give a dog to the Son of the King.

Only a fool.

5
Has Anyone Seen Polaris?

Bound by honor, duty, and obligation, the lawyer arrived in Town Square with the beagle in tow just as the sun dipped below the horizon. In his polished black briefcase were proof of his identity; his diploma from Law School; a copy of every possible chart and map, though none showed the location of Destinae; and all the money he could gather. Under his arm was tucked today's four-page newspaper, and in his hand was the leash he had purchased for the beagle. Although he had been given insufficient information and too little time, the lawyer was constrained by his vanity and his pride. Cost him what it might, he would march out of Town Square precisely as instructed, and with his dignity perfectly intact.

The beagle tugged gently on the end of her tether like a fish teasing a baited hook. The lawyer looked down. Turning her head from side to side, the beagle seemed to be inspecting the crowd that had gathered in the dusky dark.

Looking for someone.

The beagle turned and fixed her gaze firmly on the lawyer. A thought came into his mind. Gathering his courage and suspending his pride, he shouted, "Has anyone seen Polaris?" and waited to see if there would be an answer. Tick-tick-tick-tick-tick-tick-tick. The lawyer's watch was wide awake now. The only other sound was the orange and brown crackle of autumn leaves falling upon the weighty stare of the silent crowd.

Finally, "There! There is P'laris!" croaked an ancient voice in the darkening gloom. The lawyer, the beagle, and the crowd turned to face the source of the sound. It was an old farmer, pointing into the sky beyond the official clock. "There is P'laris," he shouted again, "the woon true star'a' th' north; th'only gleam in th' heavens tha' doos na' moof." Having thus spoken, the old farmer looked at the beagle. The beagle wagged her tail.

"Intellect!" boomed the voice of Judge Grey. "Are you ready to begin your journey?"

"I am here," replied the lawyer, not entirely answering the judge's question.

Judge Grey continued, "All of us are counting on you, Counselor. We trust you won't let us down."

And with no more ceremony than that, the lawyer and the beagle walked off into the darkness, guided only by a gleam in the sky.

6
Marching by Moonlight

The lawyer and the beagle had been traveling for hours in the moonlight when they came upon the cave. The beagle immediately plunged inside, sniffing as she went. Moments later, she curled up and was fast asleep before the lawyer had even opened his briefcase.

"Stupid beagle," muttered the lawyer. "There could be a bear in that cave for all she knows." Gathering a handful of small stones from the ground, the lawyer stepped quickly in front of the cave's opening and flung them hard into its deepest recesses before diving back out of the way. When no wild beast came running out, he stepped cautiously inside the cave and spread his kerchief on the cleanest patch of ground he could find. Look at her just sleeping there! he thought. That beagle has no idea how lucky she is to have me here to protect her. He opened his briefcase. Click-click. The beagle raised an eyelid and then was fast asleep again. Candles. Check. Matches. Check. The lawyer smiled in appreciation at his own preparedness. Lighting a candle, he dripped hot wax onto the top of a stone, then seated the candle firmly into it. There, that should hold you.

The cave walls danced with magical patterns.

Stepping once more into the moonlight, the lawyer picked up the heaviest rock he could lift. He wrestled it back into the cave and placed it directly atop the beagle's leash. And that should hold you, he thought. Let's see you aroo-aroo your way out of that.

"I'M C-3PO, HUMAN-CYBORG RELATIONS, AND THIS IS MY COUNTERPART, R2-D2."

7

BOOM!

BOOM! Thunder rocked the mountain and the lawyer was instantly awake. Looking toward the mouth of the cave, he saw an anxious beagle silhouetted there, backlit by flashes of lightning. Torrents of glittering rain fell hard-edged behind her. BOOM! The ground rumbled with the sound of the thunder. The beagle began to bark frantically.

"Oh, shut up!" snapped the lawyer. "It's only a thunderstorm. Go back to sleep." The beagle continued her sharp, piercing shouts. "Shut up!" the lawyer yelled; the barking only grew more urgent. Closing his eyes tightly and holding his hands over his ears, the lawyer was determined to win, but when the beagle's cold, wet nose pressed against his own, his eyes flew open in horror.

28

She had pulled her leash out from under the heavy rock. "Bark, Bark, Bark!" As he reached out to take the leash, the beagle jumped quickly away. "Bark, Bark, Bark!" She ran into the rain, stopping just outside the mouth of the cave. BOOM! The thunder rolled.

Holding his briefcase over his head like an umbrella, the lawyer stepped out of the cave and stretched out his hand to take hold of the leash. But the beagle backed away once more, barking wildly. "I'm not playing with you!" screamed the lawyer. "Get back into that cave, you stupid beagle!" Furious, he made a mad dash to grab the end of the leash.

And the hillside came roaring down behind him.

The cave where moments ago the lawyer had been sleeping was now sealed off from sunlight forever.

The lawyer was very happy to be standing in the rain.

8
In the Belly of Confusion

Throughout the night, the lawyer and the beagle marched resolutely onward. And when the storm abated, they walked onward still. Ever and ever onward they sloshed down the slope of a dripping, wooded hillside until finally, weary, wet, and sad, the lawyer stepped into a small clearing and caught a glimpse of the vast forest that lay below them.

It swallowed the horizon.

The lawyer swallowed as well, for he had never seen such a forest. Then, remembering his duty and obligation, he tightened his grip on the beagle's leash and marched directly into it.

Sunlight doesn't look like sunlight when it's filtered through dead and dying leaves. And along the edges of their shadows you will find no happy colors.

The lawyer walked until he could walk no further, then tied the beagle's leash tightly to the base of an ancient tree. He was piling dead leaves to make himself a bed when he heard a sound from deep in the throat of the beagle. She was looking into the forest behind him. He spun around; he saw nothing. "You're a very stupid beagle," he said, and went back to piling leaves.

The beagle's throat-noise then became louder and she stretched her leash tightly in his direction. Opening his briefcase, he removed the newspaper he had carried when they marched so boldly out of Town Square. He rolled it tightly and used it to spank the beagle. She didn't seem to notice.

The lawyer looked again to where the beagle was staring.

A shadowy gentleman in a formal riding coat slipped quietly from behind a tree. "Well, well, well," he said in an elegant whisper. "What business brings a man like you so deep into the Forest of Confusion?" Seeing that the lawyer was somewhat taken aback, the shadowy fellow bowed like an aristocrat and, with a calculated flourish, produced a card from his ruffled sleeve. "My name is Worry," he smiled, "and I'm here to help you."

Drawing himself quickly to his full height and straightening his clothes as best he could, the lawyer asked in his best lawyer voice, "Do you know your way through this forest?"

Worry replied softly, "Oh, but I was born in this forest."

Still tied to the tree, the beagle continued making the low, strange noise in her throat.

9
"Please allow me to introduce myself..."

"Keep a tight hold on that beagle, kind sir," said Worry as they marched deeper into the woods. "One never knows what a dog might do."

Whether it was the slowly failing daylight or the growing thickness of the forest, the lawyer did not know, but it was definitely getting darker. "Tie the dog," said Worry quietly, "and we will stop here for awhile." When the beagle was tightly secured, Worry spoke once more. "This is as far as I can take you," he smiled through thin lips, "but my partner is here to take you further." And as Worry extended his lace-cuffed wrist, a hungry, un-shaven man in ripped trousers and a grimy jacket emerged from deeper in the shadows. "Allow me intro-duce you to Fear," said Worry, "He will take things from here." And with another low bow, Worry showed his teeth and said, "Glad to have been of service to you," and drifted backwards into the trees.

"What've you got in tha' briefcase, mate?" asked Fear without the hint of a smile.

"Nothing that would interest you," replied the law-yer, tightening his grip.

"Don't be too sure about tha', mate," said Fear with a frown as he extended a bony arm toward the lawyer. "It don't take much to int'rest me. Let's see what ya got."

The beagle exploded into a cacophony of barking and leaping at the end of her leash.

"I'll do nothing of the sort!" said the lawyer, clutching the briefcase to his chest.

And then the darkness was complete.

Bowing in mock deference before the unconscious body of the lawyer, Fear sneered in cunning derision and said, "Lemme introduce you to Panic, my brother." Then, with an ugly, bad-teeth smile, Fear looked upward into the nervous face of his heavier, twitching twin and said, "Anotha' job well done."

"Grab the case and let's get outta here," replied Panic, thumping a stick into his open palm, rat-a-tat-tat. "Th' dog is makin' m' head hurt."

Fear laughed and whacked his brother on the back. "But na' as much as his head will be hurtin' inna mornin'!"

Tossing the lawyer's briefcase up into the air as they moved away, Fear and Panic were thirstily absorbed into the soft edges of darkness.

10
Nameless and Homeless

Lying motionless in the dim morning light, the lawyer slowly raised his eyelids and stared up at the high canopy of the forest. He had a headache.

Yes, a wonder of a headache. But no money, maps or matches.

No diploma to prove who he was.

But he still had his duty and obligation.

Yes, he still had those.

And a slight weight upon his chest.

Dog breath.

It was the beagle.

But why wasn't the beagle still tied to the tree?

The lawyer's struggle to sit upright made his head hurt even worse, but at least he found his answer: the beagle had chewed through her leash.

Slipping his belt from its loops around his waist, he thought he heard the beagle making that rumbling, grumbling noise again. . . . No, this time it was only his stomach, reminding him that he hadn't eaten since he left Town Square.

Ah, Town Square. . . . its newspaper stand and courthouse, its shoeshine chair and official clock. His orderly, predictable world. The only thing left of it was the thin newspaper he had rolled up to spank the beagle. Instinctively he folded it into six starched squares and placed it in the bottom left pocket of his jacket.

Using his belt again as a makeshift leash, the lawyer wrapped the rags of his dignity tightly about him and began to walk in the direction that seemed North. And as he walked, his pants dropped occasionally and exposed his bare bottom to the world.

And the leaves of the forest laughed quietly every time it happened.

11
The Terrible Truth

(IN RESPONSE TO
R2-D2'S BEEPED
AND SQUEAKED
QUESTION ABOUT
WHETHER LUKE
LIKES HIM) "NO,
I DON'T THINK HE
LIKES YOU AT ALL."
(R2 BEEPS ANOTHER
QUESTION) "NO,
I DON'T LIKE YOU
EITHER."

– C-3PO

It was difficult to tell daylight from darkness in the forest, but the lawyer knew without counting the days that they had been wandering for weeks. He knew that the nights were growing steadily colder. He knew that he and the beagle were starving.

When the lawyer had first regained consciousness, his only thought was to avoid Worry and Fear. Then, as he wandered further and further into the numbing Swamp of Depression, he began to think that even Worry and Fear might be better than no friends at all.

But yesterday the lawyer had felt the forest floor begin to rise and had allowed the slight incline to guide his footsteps in the darkness. If a step seemed easy, he knew it was leading him downward. It was only the more difficult steps that would take him higher.

Having resolved to take only the difficult steps, he sat now in bright sunlight, high upon a hilltop, scanning a panoramic forest.

A forest that seemed to have no end.

And no way out.

"Destinae does not exist," the lawyer said aloud, "and everyone who wrote of going there was telling a terrible lie." Of course they were lying. That's why their stories did not agree.

Deep in his heart, the lawyer knew that he had failed and that he was about to die.

There was only one thing left for him to do:

Free the beagle.

Stroking the dog's soft coat for the first time since he'd met her, Intellect said, "Intuition, you have been a far better friend to me than I have been to you." Then, drawing her furry cheek next to his, he whispered softly, "Go now. Run free and live."

The moment the belt was off her neck, the beagle disappeared — "Arooo! Aroo-aroo!" — out of the clearing and into the woods.

Slipping his worn belt back into its frayed loops, the lawyer had a weary thought: "Well, at least I won't die with my bare bottom showing for all the world to see." He smiled weakly into the sunlight as he lay upon the rock and remembered the clock in Town Square.

Feeling his strength beginning to fade, he whispered, "I wonder what time it is now."

12
Consolation

The lawyer stretched out shamelessly upon the stone and the sunlight warmed his skin.

He thought of the newspaper stand and laughed. He looked at his battered shoes and laughed harder still.

It felt good to laugh. He only wished the beagle were here to laugh with him.

Just then the beagle exploded through the trees as though his thoughts had called her, and in her teeth was the biggest rabbit the lawyer had ever seen. She dropped it at his feet and hung her head, panting in exhaustion.

Before the lawyer could utter a word, a burly, bearded hunter burst through the brush in exactly the spot where the beagle had appeared. Wearing a tartan plaid wool shirt and a pair of denim overalls, the hairy hunter shouted excitedly, "Ma hoonds and I were hoontin' for hare when this 'un yoomps outta the brush, and 'fore I could raise a rifle or wink, your hoond appeart outta nowhere and snatches t'hare in'er teeth on a dead run. T'were a marvelous sight, it were!" Gesturing to his own dogs, he said, "Ma hoonds and I tracked your hoond t'here." The hunter then removed his hat and, gathering such formality about himself as he could muster, asked, "Might th' wee hoond be purchased froom ya today?"

"ONCE YOU REPLACE NEGATIVE THOUGHTS WITH POSITIVE ONES, YOU'LL START HAVING POSITIVE RESULTS. WHEN I STARTED COUNTING MY BLESSINGS, MY WHOLE LIFE TURNED AROUND."

– WILLIE NELSON

"R2-D2, WHERE ARE YOU?"

– C-3PO

"Do you have a knife and matches?" asked the lawyer.

"Aye," answered the hunter anxiously. "Knife and matches I can lend, b' willya be sellin' the hoond for yoost a knife 'n' a fire?

The lawyer sat up slowly. "Friend," he said, "I can offer you only a dinner of roasted rabbit." The lawyer looked the hunter straight in the eye. "Because this beagle cannot be purchased at any price." Gathering what little strength he could muster, the lawyer wobbled to his feet and smiled. "Will you stay to dine with us?"

Looking now with grave concern at the frail lawyer and the dog, the hunter asked, "How long has't been since your last meal?" The lawyer told him their story as the hunter prepared the rabbit and the fire. When the lawyer finished speaking, the hunter remained silent for a while. Then, speaking more to himself than to the lawyer, he turned and looked with deep curiosity at the beagle. "B'why would na' a hoongry hoond a'eaten the hare instead o' bringin' it here?"

First of all, in scientific tests, dogs have proved themselves a million times more able than humans to sense certain smells. How is that possible? It's because a dog's nose has four times the volume of ours, and while a human nose contains about 5 million ethmoidal (olfactory) cells, beagles' noses have over 200 million.

Likewise, the outside of a dog's nose (especially hounds) is designed to pick up scents: large and wet, it collects and dissolves scent particles for easier identification. When a dog detects a desirable scent, it reacts by salivating, and the wet tongue also helps to pick up and dissolve more scent particles. Under perfect conditions, a beagle can easily run a line by air scenting rather than sticking its nose down close to the ground.

When a Beagler says that his or her hound is running a line, they are saying that it is following or tracking a scent trail that has been left by its intended quarry. Beagles can and have been trained to single out virtually any scent, which makes them a very versatile hound. They have been used to track rabbits/hares, squirrels, deer, coyotes, foxes, raccoons, upland game birds — also illegal drugs, bombs, natural gas leaks, combustible fuel evidence at arson scenes, and humans (search & rescue), just to name a few. Finding rabbits comes naturally to Beagles since this is what they were originally bred for. (Please note that each time I use the term rabbit, I am also talking about hares.)

– BEAGLESUNLIMITED.COM

13
The Ship Dock a'Luff

"Does this hill have a name?" asked the lawyer, licking the last taste of rabbit from his lips. Looking down, he noted with satisfaction that the beagle was still chewing on her portion.

"Epiphany is the name o' this hill," said the hunter, "and na' many can say to'a' climbed it."

"The beagle and I are going to Destinae," said the lawyer with sudden conviction. "Have you ever been there?"

The hunter answered by pointing into the sky with his hunting knife. "Followin' P'laris is surely the way to Destinae. But 'tis certain tha' noo one returns who follows tha' star."

Leaning forward into the circle of firelight, the lawyer spoke again with some intensity: "I've read of jungles and dangers and of glittering parties and uncharted seas. What have you heard of Destinae?"

"I coon tell ya only to b'ware a'the ship dock a'Luff."

"Luff?" The lawyer could not recall ever having seen Luff on any of his maps or charts. "Is Luff dangerous?"

"Aye, mos' dangerous and pow'rful is the ship dock a'Luff."

"Is there a way to get around it?"

As he whittled on a piece of wood with his hunting knife, the hunter answered quietly, "It doona' matter how far ya journey. Ya canna' escape the ship dock a'Luff if yoor plannin' to reach Destinae."

"The ship dock circles the world?" whispered the incredulous lawyer.

Thoughtful, the hunter continued, "Aye, surely Luff circles the worl', and it makes the worl' go 'roun' in circles, too."

"What kind of ships come to the ship dock of Luff?"

The hunter looked confused. "Are ya askin' about ships now?"

"Yes, what kind of ships come to the ship dock?"

Agitated, the hunter boomed, "The oonly kinda' ships there are, Lad! The ships that're carryin' wool!"

"And so all of the ships are full of wool, then?"

The hunter laughed heartily, "Noo! Th' wool is on the ships, na' in 'em. The ship dock oonly watches o'er th' ships."

Now it was the lawyer's turn to be confused.

Seeing his consternation, the hunter began to talk to him as though he were a little child. "When a little lamb b'cooms a ship, th' ship is haffin' wool on it." Pointing now at the beagle, he continued, "A ship dock is a dock that watches o'er th' ships yoos like your little bickle dock watches o'er you."

Both the hunter and the lawyer stared for a long time into the fire before the hunter continued: "Aye, Luff is pow'rful like a ship dock, and sof' and gentle like one, too."

Without removing his gaze from the flames, the lawyer answered, "And it makes the world go 'round?"

"Aye, Laddie, that it does."

When the lawyer awoke, the fire was out, the hunter was gone, and the beagle was staring northward.

"The Beagle is a gentle, sweet, lively and curious dog that just loves everyone! A happy little tail-wagger! Sociable, brave and intelligent. Calm and loving. Excellent with children and generally good with other dogs, but should not be trusted with non-canine pets. . . ."

– DOGBREEDINFO.COM

The Inner Critic is that little voice that believes you do not deserve abundant love, good health, or success. But this is only the opinion of one part of your brain — your judgmental, analytical, rational left brain. There is a whole area of your brain that doesn't make judgements at all.

Although the ability to speak and form thoughts into words and sentences rests almost exclusively with the left side of the brain, the understanding of the emotional tone of voice is a function of the right side.

Now, there's a funny thing about the right side of your brain — it is not concerned with making judgements or assessing the factual truth of a statement; that's the left brain's job. And there's yet another way in which words can sneak their message past your Inner Critic. . . . Good poets make extensive use of "right-brain language." Forget that sensible, linear, factual left-brain speech.

The language of the right brain is a horse of a different color. A riot of imagery, a cascade of connections, sensations, and associations. The right brain speaks in metaphors, juxtapositions, and similes, using a whole range of poetic devices to express the inexpressible and describe the indescribable. Emotions? No problem. Hearts soar. Lips taste like wine. Eyes are mirrors of the soul. Imagine what your left brain thinks of that. Utter nonsense! Not worth even bothering about! But to your illogical, intuitive right brain, it's perfectly clear.

– ROBIN FREDERICK, WWW.SOUNDEXP.COM

OSCAR: Then listen to me. Tonight you're going to sleep here. And tomorrow you're going to get your clothes and your electric toothbrush and you'll move in with me.

FELIX: No, no. It's your apartment. I'll be in the way.

OSCAR: There's eight rooms. We could go for a year without seeing each other. . . . Don't you understand? I want you to move in.

FELIX: Why? I'm a pest.

OSCAR: I know you're a pest, you don't have to keep telling me.

FELIX: Then why do you want me to live with you?

OSCAR: Because I can't stand living alone, that's why! . . . For crying out loud, I'm proposing to you. What do you want, a ring?

– *THE ODD COUPLE,* NEIL SIMON, 1965

"LOVE IS LIKE WILDFLOWERS — IT GROWS IN THE STRANGEST PLACES."

– UNKNOWN

14
Winter Cave of Introspection

Deep in the Forest of Confusion sits the Hill of Epiphany, and in one side of that hill is the Cave of Introspection.

It was in this cave that the lawyer and the beagle spent the winter.

Now that she was allowed to run free and unfettered, the beagle was clearly getting faster and stronger. And each evening as they sat by the fire in the cave, they would feast together on the beagle's catch of the day. What a variety of game the beagle was finding in the forest! It seemed to the lawyer that the forest was not a bit confusing to the beagle, but was truly a Forest of Opportunity.

The lawyer smiled, remembering how the hunter had refused to accept his gold watch in exchange for the hunting knife. "Noo, Laddie, the time for me is always now, an' now is a time that ne'er changes. I'm giffin' you the knife as a gift a'Luff."

Staring out of the cave and into the night, the lawyer studied the winter stars. Thinking back upon his days in Town Square, he blushed when he remembered how angry he had been when Judge Grey had insisted that their journey begin after dark. It was obvious now that the old judge clearly knew of the importance of following Polaris. But he also knew the lawyer would need to discover it for himself.

Polaris. . . .

How could all of the travelers have followed that same star, yet seen completely different things on their journeys?

When the beagle's cold nose touched his own, the lawyer spoke aloud: "Each of the stars in the sky appears to move during the night because of the rotation of the earth. . . . The fact that Polaris does not move means that it must be aligned in the heavens precisely above the earth's axis." Then his voice became a whisper when he realized the implication: "This means that everyone who has found Destinae is now sitting on top of the world."

No wonder they never returned.

15
Children of the Ship Dock

Weeks before the twins were born, the lawyer noticed the beagle growing fat and suspected that she had been cavorting with "th' ship dock a'Luff." Faith and Hope were born in the warmth of the cave during a wheezing, whistling blizzard that blustered and blew for days on end. And from the very first moment that they arrived into this world, their personalities were markedly different.

Faith, the male puppy, was courageous and quick and able. Always ready to climb or wrestle, Faith was quick to let you know he was there.

Hope, on the other hand, was cuddly and tender and loving. Much quieter and softer than her boisterous brother, Hope was drawn to where there was pain. Many a cold morning when the lawyer was feeling blue, Hope would snuggle up close beside him and nuzzle his cheek until he smiled. Meanwhile, her brother would climb a rock and bark just to show you he could do it.

To the lawyer, living with the puppies in the Cave of Introspection, the winter weeks passed like hours; whole days seemed like minutes. He had never been happier.

And when the thawing winds of spring arrived, the snow and ice were completely melted.

"You know, Lydia, I used to be a rationalist."

"What is that?"

"Well, it's sort of believing only in what you see, or hear, or feel. But lately, I've begun to suspect that there are more things in heaven and earth than I ever dreamed in my philosophy."

"You learn much when you learn that."

– COLONEL RALPH DENISTOUN TO THE GYPSY WOMAN, LYDIA, IN
PARAMOUNT'S 1947 MOVIE GOLDEN EARRINGS

16
Spring Storm

Days grew longer, buds burst on branches, and warm winds whispered of Destinae. Faith and Hope had grown strong during the short days of winter and both were wiggling to bounce into an adventure.

Intellect and Intuition knew the time had come to move on.

The forbidding Forest of Confusion was not so difficult to navigate now that the beagle was off the leash. Under logs and over brooks, across gullies and into thickets she led the lawyer and the puppies north by north, until one day, when the sun was bright and the wind sang sweetly, the forest blew away like fog and they were out of it.

Or so they thought.

A few rollicking hours of barking at butterflies and running at rainbows was all they collected before singing winds became stinging winds and rain like bullets began to fall. Soon a whistling, whipping atmosphere was sending sizable saplings sailing over their heads. The lawyer grabbed the beagles and lay face down with them in a ravine.

Snapping snakes of elec-
tricity hissed and cracked as the
sky grew as dark as midnight.
Water bullets became buckets,
and the ravine began to rumble.
Fighting his way out from under the lawyer's arm, Faith
climbed out of the ditch and onto a rock, where he
barked defiance at the storm.

And the storm barked back.

And it rained a sickness. And it rained a fear. And it rained an odor. And it rained a murder. And it rained pale eggs of the beast.

Rain fell on the towns and the fields. It fell on the tractor sheds and the labyrinth of sloughs. Rain fell on toadstools and ferns and bridges. It fell on the head of John Paul Ziller.

Rain poured for days, unceasing. Flooding occurred. The wells filled with reptiles. The basements filled with fossils. Mossy-haired lunatics roamed the dripping peninsulas. Moisture gleamed on the beak of the Raven. Ancient shamans, rained from their homes in dead tree trunks, clacked their clamshell teeth in the drowned doorways of forests. Rain hissed on the Freeway. It hissed at the prows of fishing boats. It ate the old warpaths, spilled the huckleberries, ran in the ditches. Soaking. Spreading. Penetrating.

And it rained an omen. And it rained a poison. And it rained a pigment. And it rained a seizure.

– Tom Robbins, *Another Roadside Attraction* (Random House)

17
Rain

Crawling on his elbows out of the ravine and over to the rock, the lawyer crouched behind the massive stone and tried to coax Faith off the top of it. But Faith would not be moved. The lawyer felt a sudden yank at his sleeve — Intuition was trying to get his attention. He looked back and saw that she was barking, but in the noise of the storm no sound seemed to be coming from her throat.

The ground rumbled beneath them.

In the roaring ravine where Hope had obediently remained, a mountain of water hurtled like a freight train down a track. The soundlessly screaming lawyer was scrambling leglessly toward her, arms outstretched, when a jagged jewel of light exploded like a bomb, knocking him sightless and deaf to the ground.

And in the roaring gush and rush of whirling-swirling water that pounded through the ravine, Hope was swept away. . . .

And was lost.

18
The River of Hate

When they were finally able to see again, a trembling lawyer and a muddy beagle rose shakily from the ground to survey the pointless scene.

Faith was still standing on his rock.

But Hope was nowhere to be found.

Where once had been a shallow ravine now raged a river, dirty and cold.

But it did not flow to the north.

As the lawyer watched the beagle sniff and whimper along the water's edge, he knew it was his duty to continue northward. But the beagle obviously wanted to follow the river in search of Hope. He watched her as she anxiously scoured the water's edge with Faith following close behind her.

Shrill duty demanded that they continue northward, but as the lawyer's fingers touched the buckle of his belt, he could not slip it from his waist.

No, it would not be right to leash the beagle.

"We are continuing our journey to Destinae," he shouted to no one. "We are merely taking a longer route to get there."

When Judge Grey had told him, "Your journey will take what it takes," the lawyer had assumed he was speaking of time and money.

He had never dreamed that it would take Hope.

Following Faith and Intuition, the shattered lawyer walked in silence along the river, but the absence of Hope made each footfall heavier than the last. What was this tightness in his throat, and why was his vision getting blurry? When he tripped and fell, he raised the offending stone above his head in a rage and smashed it into the face of the river with a murderous shout.

The river swallowed the stone and continued rolling on exactly as before.

But the lawyer had made his point. His vision cleared and his eyes became slits. He spat with violence into the river.

You are the river that took Hope from my life. You will be my enemy.

Forever.

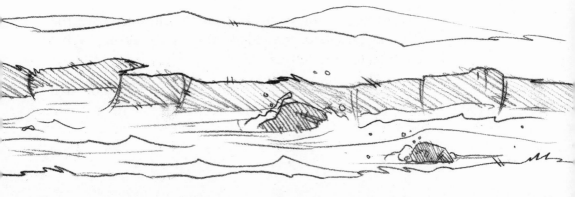

19
Village of Compromise

Early in the day, the trio traveled under spacious skies staring directly into the sun. But as morning matured into afternoon, the sun was left further and further behind until the lawyer was walking in darkness. Within just a few days, the dirty river, the staring sun, and the absence of Hope had given him such a headache that he was beginning to despair of ever completing his mission.

That's when the village appeared. Straight streets and houses with faces: a window on the left, a window on the right, and a door exactly in the middle. Pale grass and predictable yards.

The lawyer had never seen so many shades of beige.

Immediately upon the lawyer's entry into the colorless village, the beige people rushed out to wish him welcome. "We are a simple people," the mayor proclaimed with manufactured humility, "but we're more than happy to offer you such as we have to share. Fresh baked bread, cold beer, and whiskey flow in abundance here. Does it get any better than this?"

After sharing a meal of bread and beer with the friendly people of the village, the lawyer asked, "What can you tell me of Destinae?"

"Oh!" exclaimed a woman. "Destinae is not for such people as we!" It seemed to the lawyer that the woman spoke with a strange, self-righteous glee. "We are a simple folk with simple tastes who have learned to be content with such things as Nature has chosen to give."

"And what has Nature seen fit to give?" asked the lawyer.

"All that can be made from grain," replied a man boldly from the middle of the group. "Look 'round about you at the fields," he continued proudly. "What other village has such an abundance of grain as we have here in Compromise?"

Yes, an abundance of bread — with plenty of beer and whiskey — could go a long way toward keeping a village contented.

No, living in Compromise wouldn't be such a bad life.

Not a bad life at all.

20
Contentment in the Village

The lawyer had been in the village for only a few days when he began to seriously consider discontinuing the journey. After all, many of the people here in the village did not even believe in Destinae. And some of their arguments were rather convincing.

Day after day the lawyer asked questions and was given answers. But as the days wore on, his questions became fewer and fewer.

One day the lawyer asked one of his new friends where he might find some wine — and was surprised at the offended answer: "To make wine would require much fruit!" Staring at the clearly insane lawyer, the friend added, "And we do not bear much fruit in Compromise."

But the lawyer wasn't insane. He wasn't even unfriendly. He was simply a lawyer. And as such, he chose to press the matter further: "Have you never considered growing fruit along with the grain here in your fertile fields? Fruit would add variety to your menu and provide much-needed vitamins for the health of the village. I believe that adding fruit should be discussed."

"If Nature had wanted us to have fruit, she would have placed our village on the other side of the Purple Mountains."

The lawyer persisted: "But can you not simply journey to the other side of the mountains and bring back such fruit as grows there? The mountains are only two miles away."

"You have only recently come into our village," his friend answered with stiff finality, "so you do not yet know our ways. But you must learn to leave well enough alone."

And his friend walked angrily away.

Late that night, the lawyer, Intuition, and Faith were sitting at the northern edge of the village staring into the sky above the Purple Mountains when Intuition's ears suddenly twitched and she cocked her head as though listening.

Just then, the town's elderly mayor arrived and sat down next to the lawyer. "You asked a foolish question today," said the mayor. "You're still considered a new-comer to our village, and therefore the people have cho-sen to forgive you. But in the future, you'll be expected to behave more like one of us."

"Well, since I am technically still a newcomer," said the lawyer, "may I ask just one last question?"

"Certainly," said the mayor with a smile.

The lawyer looked deep into the old man's eyes and asked, "How did you come to be here?"

21

"Aroo! Aroo-aroo!"

"Aroo! Aroo-aroo!" wailed Intuition. "Aroo! Aroo-aroo!" echoed Faith. And then the two beagles shot across the grain fields like arrows fired from a bow.

"Aroo! Aroo-aroo!" Their voices were already surprisingly distant.

"Aroo! Aroo-aroo!" Now their song could barely be heard at all.

"Well, young fellow," began the mayor slowly, as though he were about to bestow great wisdom upon the lawyer, "like you, I once was a believer in Destinae, and back in those days we. . . ."

The lawyer wasn't really sure what the old man said after that. The mayor droned on and on about hard work and bad luck while the lawyer strained to hear the beagles in the distance. The lawyer didn't want to seem unfriendly, so every once in a while he would nod his head and say, "Hmm. . . ." as though pondering what the old man was saying. Finally, after what seemed nearly an hour, Intuition returned and began barking frantically at him.

These weren't the "Aroos" of a chase. This was nothing less than a cacophony of barking and leaping, like the one she had delivered from the end of her leash when he had fought with Fear in the Forest of Confusion. There was only one thing it could mean!

The lawyer leaped to his feat as the mayor concluded, ". . . and that was when we lost hope."

Beaming a great smile at the dignified old gent, the lawyer screamed in anguished delight, "You should have had a beagle!" Then he began running as hard as he could, following Intuition as she scampered back toward the Purple Mountains.

They were barely halfway there when the lawyer heard the voices of the twins not far ahead. "Aroo! Aroo!" they sang triumphantly. "Aroo! Aroo-aroo!" answered their mother. "Aroo!" shouted the lawyer, laughing.

The four collided in a furry ball of hugs and sweat and laughter and tears and dog breath, and they rolled ridiculously together on the ground. Finally, exhausted, they collapsed in the field and lay snuggled happily together. That night the lawyer dreamed great and colorful dreams with three smelly dogs amidst the amber waves of grain.

22
Climbing
the Purple Mountains

They were halfway up the Purple Mountains when the slope grew steeper and it became clear to the lawyer what had happened to Hope.

After the storm, when she had found herself beached on the shore of the dirty river, Hope had assumed that the troupe would continue northward and, under this assumption, had chased Polaris until she came to the Purple Mountains. Halfway up, she had begun to call for her companions, and her mother and brother had heard.

Oh, Hope, how you ease the journey!

It had been a long afternoon of jagged rocks, perilous ledges, slippery slopes, and unsure toeholds when the reunited team finally achieved the crest of the Purple Mountains. Gathering the three beagles into his arms, the lawyer sat and looked down, down, down to the contented village of Compromise.

It frightened him that he had almost stayed there.

Yes, in that colorless place could be found plenty of bread, beer, and whiskey — but no fruit, no wine, no dreams.

A sympathetic tear fell off the lawyer's chin. He sighed deeply and said, "They don't even know what they're missing."

A series of sharp, piercing shouts from Intuition jolted him out of his reverie. The lawyer remembered this bark from the night of the avalanche, when he was in danger of being trapped and suffocated in the cave. He looked quickly at the beagle and saw that she was staring intently down at the town below.

"Yes, Intuition, I understand," said the lawyer, "and I most wholeheartedly agree."

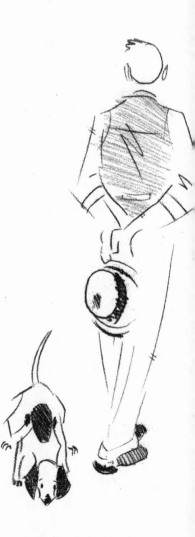

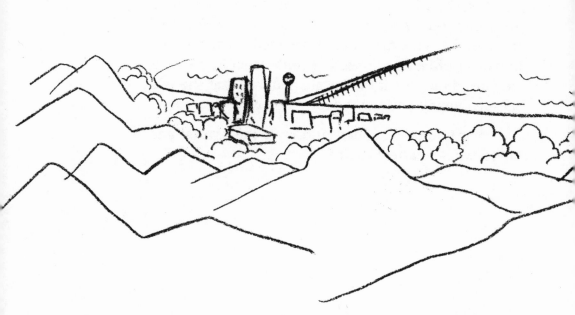

23
Across the Fruited Plain

Looking now toward the north from the crest of the Purple Mountains, the wide-eyed lawyer gazed in wonder at a sight more glorious than anything he had ever seen. In the distance was a shining sea. Stretching all the way to the shore was a vibrant plain exploding in color — apples, oranges, grapes, bananas, pears, mangos, coconuts, pineapples, tomatoes, avocados, and plums in such abundance that they could not be counted.

And where the plains met the shore, there appeared to be a city.

Surely this was Destinae!

The troupe ran, jumped, and tumbled down the mountainside and onto the fruited plains. But the plains turned out to be far broader than they had seemed from the top of the mountain, and now it was getting dark. Excited, the lawyer lay under the branches of a commiphora tree and drank of its sweet perfume.

Looking at the stars, the lawyer realized that his theory had obviously been wrong. With Destinae so very near to them, Polaris should be directly overhead.

But it wasn't.

Evidently, Destinae did not sit at the top of the world.

24
Ocean of Tears

As the lawyer neared the seaside town, he was greeted by the smell of a dank and salty ocean that stretched as far as he could see. High above that ocean, a proud and majestic ship dock jutted nearly a mile out to sea from the water's edge. And on this dock surged a restless ocean of anxious, uneasy people — back and forth, shoreward and then seaward, never at rest.

This was a strange and unusual place.

The crowd on the ship dock contained every type of person the lawyer had ever seen: athletes and writers, sculptors and singers, musicians carrying instruments, painters toting easels. Although none were actually writing, sculpting, painting, or singing, the lawyer noted that each looked quite ready to do so should he ever be asked to begin. He saw borrowers and bankers, gamblers and investors, ministers and politicians — each pacing intently back and forth, going nowhere.

"These people certainly have more energy than the ones living in the village of Compromise, but they don't seem quite as friendly," said the lawyer to the beagles. "But we shall see what we can see."

Unlike the friendly villagers of Compromise, no one here spoke to the lawyer at all except to ask if he had "connections" or knew "the name of a good agent." Finally, the lawyer stopped a stylishly dressed man and asked, "Do you know the way to Destinae?" Without a word, the man spun around and pointed to a small building on the highest level of the ship dock. Above the building was a large sign: "TICKETS TO DESTINAE."

"Thank you," shouted the lawyer as he quickly began climbing the steps.

When he had finally reached the dizzying level of the ticket booth, he gasped, "Why is this ship dock built so high above the water?"

Suddenly everyone wanted to talk. "Because of the size and splendor of the ships that dock here," the people told him excitedly. And for the next two hours, the lawyer listened to dozens of exciting stories of ships taking people away in splendor to Destinae.

25
A Ticket to Ride

"So what do I do next?" queried the lawyer. "How much do these tickets cost?"

"Tickets carry all kinds of prices," answered the man staring directly into his face, "but the secret is to have a winning one."

"A winning ticket?" asked the lawyer, befuddled.

"Yes," the man answered with a knowing wink. "You've got to have the right combination."

And quickly and quietly, the crowd that had gathered around him began to disperse.

"How often does the ship come?" asked the lawyer to the backs of their vanishing heads.

"Most of us have been waiting all our lives," answered a voice in the distance.

"But good things come to those who wait," responded another automatically.

Not quite knowing what else to do, the lawyer began pacing the ship dock along with the people who were waiting for their ship to come in.

But he was troubled by an itch in his brain.

He smiled as he remembered the hunter on the hilltop of Epiphany. Wouldn't the "hoonter" laugh if he knew that there really was a "ship dock" on the way to Destinae!

For a moment, the lawyer thought he had scratched the itch — but no, it was still there in his mind. Dangling his feet off the edge of the ship dock and looking into the beagles' faces, the lawyer spoke in quiet reflection: "In all the accounts I've read of journeys to Destinae, not one of them ever mentioned agents or cruises or lottery tickets. And the only one who spoke of an ocean wrote of sailing uncharted waters in an open boat."

Intuition just watched him and waited. Hope crawled up into his lap.

Then the lawyer remembered the maps. Yes, it was the memory of a map that was itching in his mind — a map with a broad body of water at the top of it, marking the farthest that anyone had ever journeyed and returned. What was the name of that sea? The itch grew worse than ever. He closed his eyes to concentrate. Seeing his distress, Hope placed her paws on his chest and touched her nose to his to let him know she was there. Smiling, he muttered, "Hope, what would I ever do without you?"

The lawyer's eyes flew open. That was it! The name on the map!

This was the Sea of False Hope.

26
The Leap of Faith

SPLASH! Faith leaped off the end of the ship dock and began swimming toward the north. Immediately, Intuition launched herself into the water in pursuit.

The lawyer assumed that Intuition would quickly catch up to Faith and bring him back unharmed, so he was more than a little alarmed when he saw Intuition take the lead and continue swimming northward.

"Intuition! Faith!" The dogs just kept on swimming.

When he finally realized what was happening, the lawyer scooped Hope into his arms and leaped out over the water. . . .

Only to learn that it was barely four feet deep.

Holding Hope to his chest and walking as fast as he could, the lawyer followed in the wake of Faith and Intuition. The water grew deeper — up to his chest, then up to his nose. When the water got to be a little higher than his head, the lawyer held Hope above him and bounced along the bottom, gulping air each time his head bobbed above the water.

By the time the water began to grow shallower, the lawyer was nearly exhausted. When it was down to his chest, he stopped and turned to face the city. The ship dock could no longer be seen. Turning slowly in a circle, the lawyer saw nothing but water in every direction. It reminded him of the endless Forest of Confusion that he had seen from the hilltop of Epiphany.

When he finally reached water that was only waist-deep, the lawyer caught up to Faith and Intuition. Finding the older beagle nearly exhausted, he picked her up and carried her on his shoulders. But young Faith seemed to be swimming more strongly than ever.

Following Faith's lead as the pup swam doggedly toward the north, the lawyer was more thankful than ever that the puppies had been born.

27
Knee Deep

Hours later, with darkness falling, the lawyer found himself in water only two feet deep, but there was still no land on the horizon.

Polaris, however, was nearly overhead.

Now fully rested, Intuition leaped into the water as the lawyer picked up Faith and laid him dripping across his shoulders. There had been nothing to eat since the Fruited Plain, and this water wasn't drinkable. In the darkness, the lawyer could feel invisible sea creatures brushing against his legs. And even though the water was shallow, it was still too deep to let him lie down and rest.

Hungry, thirsty, tired, the lawyer held Hope close to his chest and waded onward into the night.

"If I could give you but one gift, my friend, it would be the gift to see yourself as others see you. Then you would realize how truly special you are."

– UNKNOWN

28
Diamonds of a Princess

The ocean's surface glittered in the morning sun like diamonds in the necklace of a princess. But the water was getting neither shallower nor deeper. It remained eternally two feet deep. The lawyer's hips ached from his constant struggle against it, and he wished with all his heart that he could lie down. But the water was still too deep.

As the sun rose into the sky, the water's pretty glitter became a hard glare. No sleep and too much sunlight caused the lawyer's eyes to swell. They were now nearly closed.

By late afternoon, he couldn't see at all.

Blindly following the sounds of Faith and Intuition as they took turns leading the way north, the lawyer held Hope close to his chest (she was never allowed to lead — no one quite trusted her sense of direction).

When the lawyer could no longer feel the warmth of the sun on his skin, he knew that night had fallen. His sun-glared eyes were feeling better, but his paper throat was crackling with thirst.

After midnight, the water seemed to be getting shallower. The lawyer had been in the sea for nearly forty hours when he suddenly realized that he was on dry land. He stopped walking. Gently he set the beagles on the earth. He opened his exhausted eyes — and was overjoyed to find that his sight had returned.

Ahead of him, a multicolored aurora of light seemed to rise out of the ground, and the lawyer was drawn magnetically toward it.

He looked up — and saw that Polaris was directly overhead.

29
Destinae!

"TOTO . . . I HAVE
A FEELING WE'RE
NOT IN KANSAS
ANY MORE."

– DOROTHY

As he came closer to it, the lawyer saw that the colorful aurora was no less than a mighty fountain of light spraying up and out in every direction without ever making a sound.

A salty lawyer and three weary beagles waded into it and found it good.

How long they splashed and drank from the fountain, no one really knew. But when they emerged from it, their only thought was to rest.

The lawyer lay himself down and went to sleep on a park bench that was strangely familiar yet seemed somehow out of place. The beagles circled the bench as though on guard, then lay down quietly beneath it and took turns keeping watch during the night.

Poindexter was nowhere in sight.

"You have noticed that everything an Indian does is in a circle, and that is because the Power of the World always works in circles, and everything tries to be round. . . . The Sky is round, and I have heard that the earth is round like a ball, and so are all the stars. The wind, in its greatest power, whirls. Birds make their nest in circles, for theirs is the same religion as ours. . . . Even the seasons form a great circle in their changing, and always come back again to where they were. The life of a man is a circle from childhood to childhood, and so it is in everything where power moves."

– BLACK ELK, OGLALA SIOUX HOLY MAN, 1863-1950

30
Town Without a Square

The lawyer and the beagles awoke to the beginning of a brand new day. In the warm glow of early morning they could see that their fountain of color sat precisely at the top of the world. And around the fountain ran a circular road, with other roads radiating from it like the spokes of a wheel. And along those roads were lights and colors and wonders that could not be described — soldiers without uniforms, books without covers, buildings without ceilings or walls.

The lawyer stared long and curiously at all of this until the truth finally peeked over the horizon of his mind: Destinae doesn't have a town square but is built in a perfect circle. And instead of a ticking, official clock, Destinae has a fountain at its heart.

Looking back at the park bench that he had laid himself down on, the lawyer noticed for the first time an elegant sign on a pole behind it: "Birthplace of the King." And while he was standing and staring at it, hundreds of people flooded into the square.

Many of them warmly shouted to him and to the beagles, "Welcome to Destinae!"

31
End of the Line

It was the proudest moment of his life.

And the most cruel.

The lawyer had completed his assignment, fulfilled his mission, and successfully guarded the gift his town had sent to the Son of the King. But how was he going to explain the puppies?

More important, how was he going to live without the beagles?

Would the King's son let him visit them?

Would he be allowed to remain in Destinae?

The only thing he knew for certain was that the King's son could not possibly be worthy of so great a gift. But Intuition had already been given to him by the citizens of Town Square, for on her collar plate was clearly engraved, "A Gift for the Son of the King."

But what about the puppies?

The lawyer felt that if he lost Hope again he would surely die.

People were suddenly all around him, preparing a banquet in the circle. But the lawyer's vision was getting blurry again, and he felt that same odd tightness in his throat that he had felt alongside the river.

He quickly chose a road leading out of town and hurried down it — with all three beagles.

"Not everything we are capable of knowing and doing is accessible to or expressible in language. This means that some of our personal knowledge is off limits even to our own personal thoughts! Perhaps this is why humans are so often at odds with themselves, because there is more going on in our minds than we can ever consciously know."

– DR. RICHARD E. CYTOWIC, M.D., NEUROLOGIST

32
Taking the Road Not Taken

Sitting in a field freshly wounded by the ripping steel of a plow, the lawyer watched a plaid-shirted farmer sowing seed in soft silence. He thought of all the things he should say to the beagle.

But he didn't say any of them, because the beagle already knew.

When the farmer came to the place where the lawyer was sitting, he said, "Seed's a foony thing is seed. If ya doona giff it up and let i' go, it canna' b'coom wha'twas meant to be."

The lawyer smiled a bittersweet smile as he remembered his old friend, the hunter. After dusting himself off and wiping the damp from his cheeks, the lawyer stood up to speak to the farmer — but the farmer was nowhere to be found.

So the lawyer just took a deep breath and held it.

And squeezed his eyes shut tight.

A few minutes later, when the lawyer was breathing and seeing again, he and the beagles began their lonely march back into town.

As they came within sight of the circle, Intuition moved into a position directly in front of the lawyer and the puppies fell in on either side of him. So stately were the lawyer and the beagles as they marched in procession that the crowds parted to let them pass.

But the lawyer didn't notice any of this.

His vision had gone blurry again.

33
Meeting the Son of the King

The lawyer's shins bumped into something. He cleared his eyes and looked down to see that it was only Intuition. Evidently she had stopped when she reached the road that circled the silent fountain.

Looking up, the lawyer saw food and flowers and people packed into the circle. Every eye, however, was riveted on the smiling King as he stood before the fountain. His royal voice boomed, "Hear me all!" and the people grew as quiet as the calm before a storm.

"Today we receive the messenger who has guarded that which is closest to our heart." The King extended a hand toward the spot where the lawyer was standing. Every eye in the city looked at him.

The lawyer was supposed to do something now. But what?

When the silence had become unbearable, the lawyer took a faltering step forward and in his best voice said, "Allow me to present to you the gift that was entrusted to me when I left the people of Town Square."

Upon hearing these words, the citizens of Destinae went wild with clapping and cheering. But the lawyer raised his hand to silence them, for he had more to say.

His voice rang out with newfound authority: "I have a request to make of the Son of the King."

The people gasped in loud surprise. But from over near the fountain, the King's deep voice boomed once more across the circle: "And what might this request be?"

"During the winter the beagle found Love, and these two puppies were born unto her," said the lawyer. "I ask only that the messenger might be allowed to keep the puppies."

After a moment's pause, the King replied, "The puppies, of course, will always belong to the messenger. But they are Love's gift to the Son of the King."

Seeing the lawyer's confusion, the beagle pressed her nose against his bottom left jacket pocket, then raised her eyes to meet his. Reaching inside the pocket, the lawyer found the newspaper he had folded and placed there months ago. He pulled it out and read the headline again: "King's Son to Be Tested."

Then, for the first time since he had picked it up from the newspaper stand on the morning that their journey began, the lawyer read the story beneath the headline: "Given only a single day to prepare, the King's Lost Son must journey alone to Destinae to prove that he is prepared to inherit the kingdom. Fearful of the many perils that await him, the people of Destinae have sent him the gift of a magical beagle messenger to guard and guide him on his way."

And as he continued to stare at the newspaper, the King's son could hear the voices of three beagles singing in perfect harmony: "Aroo! Aroo-aroo! Aroo! Aroo-aroo! Aroo! Aroo-aroo!

And the people of Destinae clapped and shouted in rhythm with the beagle's song: "Welcome home! Welcome home! Welcome home!"

And thus it was, with the magical beagle of Intuition at his side, that Prince Intellect began to learn about the kingdom that his father had prepared for them before he was even born.

And all these things happened in the days when Faith and Hope were very young.

THIS IS THE ONLY
KNOWN PHOTO OF
THE LAWYER WITH
THE BEAGLE, TAKEN
DURING THEIR
WINTER AT THE
CAVE OF INTROSPECTION.

In Search of the Beagle

On January 7, 2002, six people met in one of the three private dining rooms of the Waldorf-Astoria's famous Peacock Alley restaurant: a publisher, a neurologist, an army chaplain, a businesswoman, a motivational speaker, and a literary critic. The following is a transcript of their roundtable discussion.

RAY BARD: Okay, the tape recorder is now on. But before we begin, is there anything else that anyone would like from the kitchen?

TALYA MADORA: Another glass of this wine?

DR. DARCY DA SILVA: Me too.

PAULINE LEPINE: And me.

RAY BARD: Bring two bottles. While he's getting that, I'll introduce today's worldwide panel of experts for the transcript. Starting on my left, we have Dr. Darcy da Silva, a neurologist from the International Institute of Biophysics. Seated next to her is Chaplain Jim Chaney of the U.S. Army, and next to the good chaplain is Talya Madora, cofounder of Allura Cosmetics. Did I overhear you saying a moment ago that you had sold the company?

TALYA MADORA: Yes, Celine and I both felt it was time for a new challenge.

RAY BARD: I think most people have heard the story of how you launched the company with almost no money, so would it be out of line for me to ask the selling price?

TALYA MADORA: We sold it for just over 40 million dollars; they wanted our process patents.

RAY BARD: Congratulations.

TALYA MADORA: Thank you.

DINK WEBER: Now that I know who I'm sitting next to, I think I might need a glass of that wine myself.

RAY BARD: And next to Ms. Madora sits motivational speaker and author Dr. Dink Weber.

DINK WEBER: I'm delighted to have been invited.

RAY BARD: And finally we have Pauline Lepine, one of America's best-known literary critics. Pauline, let's begin with you. What did you think of *Free the Beagle*?

PAULINE LEPINE: Are you sure you want to start with me?

RAY BARD: We've got to start somewhere.

PAULINE LEPINE: Okay. But I don't really think you're going to want to hear this.

RAY BARD: Sure we do. Just tell us what you thought.

PAULINE LEPINE: I found the book to be shallow, obvious, and derivative; at best, it's a bad rewrite of *The Wizard of Oz*.

RAY BARD: Do you really think so?

PAULINE LEPINE: It's the textbook allegorical Hero's Journey, updated for a new generation. But this is a story that has already been told by some of the greatest writers in history.

TALYA MADORA: But wouldn't you agree that the story needed to be updated to make it more accessible and relevant to modern readers?

RAY BARD: Pauline, are you suggesting that perhaps the final hero's journey has already been made?

PAULINE LEPINE: Liza Minnelli, when asked to sing "Somewhere Over the Rainbow," replied as your author should have replied: "That song has already been sung." Homer was the first to sing it in the *Odyssey*. Apollonius sang it in *Jason and the Argonauts*. John Bunyan sang it in *Pilgrim's Progress*. Tolkien sang it in *The Lord of the Rings*. George Lucas sang it in *Star Wars,* and most certainly Frank Baum sang it in *The Wizard of Oz*.

RAY BARD: Why do you emphasize *The Wizard of Oz*?

PAULINE LEPINE: Instead of Dorothy and Toto, we're given a lawyer and a beagle. Instead of Glenda the good witch, we have the unnamed hunter. And instead of the scarecrow and the tin man, we've got the puppies, Faith and Hope. Frankly, I couldn't find an original thought anywhere in the story.

RAY BARD: Ouch.

PAULINE LEPINE: Chapter 7 and chapter 29 both begin with direct quotes from *The Wizard of Oz*. Obviously, this writer had Oz rattling around in his brain the entire time he was writing. And isn't this the same author who wrote *The Wizard of Ads*? Ads, Oz. How much more proof do you need?

RAY BARD: Fair enough. What did the rest of you think when you read the story? What did you think the book was about?

DINK WEBER: We'd like to know what you thought it was about. You're the publisher.

RAY BARD: All I can say is that it's an adventure story about a lawyer and a beagle on a journey. Anything beyond that, you people are going to have to tell me.

DINK WEBER: I think it was about tenacity and perseverance. Believing in yourself. Not giving up. Overcoming adversity.

RAY BARD: So what was your favorite part, Dink?

DINK WEBER: I'd have to say it's when the lawyer and the beagle are lost in the darkness of the Swamp of Depression and the lawyer finally figures out how to get them out of it.

RAY BARD: Which was . . . ?

DINK WEBER: By taking the hard steps. Like the book says, easy steps take us downward. It's only the hard steps that lift us higher. To get out of a low place, we've got to overcome the suction and the gravity of our own bad habits. We've got to take the hard steps. I thought it was a great book.

TALYA MADORA: Me, too. There were a number of times when I said, "Wow. I didn't know that that ever happened to anyone but me." Anyone who's thinking of going into business definitely needs to read this book.

RAY BARD: Any parts in particular?

TALYA MADORA: They should read the whole thing. It's all good.

RAY BARD: So when was the first time you said, "I never knew that things like this ever happened to anyone but me?"

TALYA MADORA: I would say it was probably at the very beginning, when the lawyer was pressed for time and was running down the checklist in his mind. I've felt that way nearly every morning of my life. And I loved all the symbols.

RAY BARD: What symbols do you mean?

TALYA MADORA: Was it just me, or did anyone else think the newspaper stand stood for information and the shoeshine chair for vanity?

CHAPLAIN CHANEY: The shoeshine chair and the lawyer's shoes were definitely symbols of vanity, because when the lawyer thinks he's about to die, he looks at his worn-out shoes and laughs. A man on his deathbed will often see vanity as bitterly comic, somehow.

TALYA MADORA: "Vanity of vanities. All is vanity." The words of the son of David, king in Jerusalem. Ecclesiastes chapter one.

CHAPLAIN CHANEY: I'm impressed.

DINK WEBER: But the other big image in the opening chapter was the official clock in the center of Town Square, which obviously stands for the passing of time. And what about the starched handkerchief the lawyer places directly over his heart? And the reference to Holly Golightly? And the fact that there is no map to Destinae?

TALYA MADORA: Yes! That was the second time I said, "Wow. This author is definitely a person who has started a business." Because there is never a map to Destinae. Success is always about learning to improvise.

RAY BARD: So who, or what, is Poindexter?

TALYA MADORA: Poindexter is every distraction that makes us stray from our chosen path. Poindexter is unexpected trouble.

PAULINE LEPINE: A little like the Wicked Witch of the West, perhaps?

DINK WEBER: Sure, you could use that metaphor. But to me, Poindexter is negative thinking. We've all got to learn to overcome our own negative thoughts.

CHAPLAIN CHANEY: I saw Poindexter as an emissary of the enemy.

DINK WEBER: You mean like a demon?

CHAPLAIN CHANEY: Yes, exactly.

RAY BARD: When did you first begin seeing Poindexter as a demon, Chaplain Chaney?

CHAPLAIN CHANEY: It was near the end of the book when the lawyer lay down on the park bench to go to sleep and all three beagles stayed awake to keep an eye out for Poindexter. It made me think of John chapter 10 where Jesus says, "The thief comes only to steal and kill and destroy. But I have come that they may have life, and have it to the full." Intuition, Faith, and Hope were sent to guard the Son of the King against the thief, the enemy of his soul. The beagles knew that even if he hadn't shown his face in awhile, the thief was still out there somewhere.

RAY BARD: But if the dogs were guarding the Son of the King from demons, does that mean that you're seeing the lawyer as Jesus and the dogs as angels?

CHAPLAIN CHANEY: No. It is we who are the sons of the king. "For all who are being led by the Spirit of God, these are sons of God." Romans 8. It was to us that God gave the gifts of intuition, faith, and hope.

TALYA MADORA: That brings up another interesting point. Doesn't the Christian Bible say something about faith, hope, and love? "And the greatest of these is love?"

CHAPLAIN CHANEY: First Corinthians 13.

TALYA MADORA: So why wasn't there a third puppy named Love?

CHAPLAIN CHANEY: Faith and Hope were the children of Love. Remember the hunter and the Sheep Dog of Love? It was only after the beagle found Love that Faith and Hope were born. Without love, there is no faith and there is no hope.

TALYA MADORA: I get it.

RAY BARD: Dr. da Silva? We haven't heard from you yet.

DR. DARCY DA SILVA: I can only say that I am finding these interpretations to be utterly fascinating. If you don't mind, I'd like to save my own thoughts for a while longer and just continue to listen.

RAY BARD: Okay. But we definitely want to hear from you.

DR. DARCY DA SILVA: Oh, don't worry, you will.

RAY BARD: Talya, you were telling us about the different times you said, "Wow. I never knew that anyone but me ever felt this way." Can you think of another time you had that thought while reading the story?

TALYA MADORA: Yes. Here at the end of chapter 10, right after the lawyer is mugged by Panic and Fear. "Using his belt again as a makeshift leash, the lawyer wrapped the rags of his dignity tightly about him and began to walk in the direction that seemed North. And as he walked, his pants dropped occasionally and exposed his bare bottom to the world. And the leaves of the forest laughed quietly every time it happened." Been there. Done that.

RAY BARD: Elaborate on that for us.

TALYA MADORA: Well, few things in business are as humiliating as those times when you get nervous, and panic, and do something stupid. And afterwards, you always feel like the whole world is watching and laughing at you. You feel naked. And the story doesn't say that the lawyer "walked north," but that he walked "in the direction that seemed North." That spoke to me, too, because when you get disoriented like that it's hard to know for sure when you're finally back on track. You've just got to take the direction that "feels" right.

RAY BARD: Are there any other times the book spoke to you as an entrepreneur?

TALYA MADORA: Oh sure. Lots.

RAY BARD: Can you give us another example?

TALYA MADORA: Here in chapter 7, where the lawyer narrowly escapes being sealed in the cave by an avalanche. The chapter ends with the words, "The lawyer was very happy to be standing in the rain." That reminded me of the times I've escaped disaster through sheer dumb luck. And each time it happened, I was very happy that Allura hadn't gone under, even though we were still in very difficult circumstances. It felt good to still be standing, so to speak, even though we were standing in the rain.

DR. DARCY DA SILVA: I am sorry, but as you know, I am not from this country, so I must ask: When you used the words "dumb luck" just now, what did you mean?

TALYA MADORA: Dumb luck. You know. Stupid, inexplicable good fortune.

DR. DARCY DA SILVA: I see.

RAY BARD: Why do you ask, Dr. da Silva? What did you think she might have meant?

DR. DARCY DA SILVA: I thought she was using the word "dumb" as in "mute" or "unable to speak."

RAY BARD: Let's suppose she had said "mute luck" instead of "dumb luck." What would have been the significance of that?

DR. DARCY DA SILVA: Allow me to answer you later, please. Right now I am still just listening.

DINK WEBER: I sure wish you'd tell us now. You've got me on pins and needles here.

RAY BARD: Have you found another example, Talya?

TALYA MADORA: Chapter 19, "Village of Compromise."

RAY BARD: Why was this chapter significant to you?

TALYA MADORA: The village of Compromise would never have been on the route of the lawyer if he had continued to follow his dream. It's only when we quit following our star that we find ourselves in the drab place of the beige people.

RAY BARD: Give us an example of what you mean.

TALYA MADORA: American automakers. In the 1970s, they quit following their star and made a long series of disastrous compromises. The result was drab cars for beige people. The leader,

General Motors, said, "Instead of designing different cars for Chevrolet, Pontiac, Oldsmobile, Buick, and Cadillac, why don't we just use the same few platforms for all our brands and then differentiate them by painting them different colors and installing different front grilles, taillights, and interiors in each brand?" In the short run, it looked like genius. But it only took a few years for the public to realize that American carmakers had lost their way. That's when we opened our hearts and our wallets to all the exciting new imports from overseas — cars made by people still following their star. That's what the quality movement and customer service movement during the past couple of decades was all about: following your star and not settling for second best.

RAY BARD: You really like that chapter, don't you?

TALYA MADORA: Yes, I feel it's profound. Chapter 19 is also the part that relates today's America to the patriotic song.

RAY BARD: Explain.

TALYA MADORA: The opening sentence of chapter 19 mentions "spacious skies," and Compromise is bordered all around by "amber waves of grain," and to the north are the majestic "purple mountains" above the "fruited plain."

CHAPLAIN CHANEY: "America, America, God shed his grace on thee."

DINK WEBER: "And crown thy good with brotherhood, from sea to shining sea."

TALYA MADORA: And then at the end of chapter 22, when they're all on top of the mountain looking down at the village of Compromise, Intuition begins barking just like she did when the lawyer was in danger of being trapped and suffocated in the cave. Business is like that. When you're stuck in compromise instead of following your dream, you feel like you're trapped and suffocating.

DINK WEBER: Tell it, sister.

RAY BARD: Chaplain Chaney, did you want to expand on Talya's interpretation?

CHAPLAIN CHANEY: I just wanted to say that if you were to draw a map of their journey with north at the top, the village of

Compromise would be below the purple mountains and the fruited plains would be above them. This speaks not only of the lyrics in the song, but also of the lower and upper middle classes in America.

RAY BARD: Tell us what you mean.

CHAPLAIN CHANEY: Those who are frightened by the obstacle of the Purple Mountains are the ones who stay in Compromise and are sated "with all that can be made from grain." Now look closely there, in chapter 22, where Talya was just reading. It says, "Yes, in that colorless place could be found plenty of bread, beer, and whiskey — but no fruit, no wine, no dreams."

DINK WEBER: You're not going to tell us that has something to do with the Bible, are you?

CHAPLAIN CHANEY: Well, no, but now that you mention it, it was a quest for grain that led eleven of the sons of Israel into Egypt, or Compromise, and it was there that they found the twelfth brother, Joseph, whom they had earlier sold into slavery for dreaming dreams. But Joseph the dreamer didn't dream any dreams in Egypt, he only interpreted the dreams of others.

DINK WEBER: What about the fruit and the wine? It seems to me that you're making some pretty vague connections here, chaplain. And I don't think you can make all the symbols fit your explanation. And like Johnny Cochran says, "If it doesn't fit, you must acquit."

CHAPLAIN CHANEY: Wine, throughout the Bible, is used as a type, or symbol, of the Spirit of God, and Jesus often talked about the fruits of the Spirit. And as the beagle story tells us, neither of these is found in abundance when you're living in Compromise. I'm telling you, the author is a Bible scholar. No question about it. And I could show you a dozen examples more specific than these.

RAY BARD: Such as?

CHAPLAIN CHANEY: Surely it didn't escape your notice that the King was born in humble circumstances directly beneath a star? And what is the park bench if not a substitute for the manger? And what is Polaris if not the star of Bethlehem? I believe *Free the Beagle* is a story about the relentless search of a person who wants to know God in a personal way. The author might as well have ended the story with Jeremiah 29:13: "And you will seek me and find me when you search for me with all your heart."

DINK WEBER: Yes, Polaris has certain similarities to the Star of Bethlehem, but taken literally, Polaris represents one of mankind's greatest scientific triumphs.

RAY BARD: How so, Dr. Weber?

DINK WEBER: When sailors learned to use Polaris to navigate, it was a scientific breakthrough that allowed contact between widely separated peoples and stimulated the growth of commerce. This also ties in with Talya's business interpretation, since the pole star allowed humanity to safely and reliably transport goods and services over long distances.

PAULINE LEPINE: Ray, did these people read the same story I read?

RAY BARD: The cover letter warned you that the story was "deceptively simple," Pauline.

PAULINE LEPINE: I'm going to have to start reading my cover letters a lot more closely.

RAY BARD: So what were your favorite parts of this book, Dink?

DINK WEBER: Chapter 8. Fourth paragraph. "Sunlight doesn't look like sunlight when it's filtered through dead and dying leaves. And along the edges of their shadows you will find no happy colors."

RAY BARD: Why did that particular segment ring true for you, Dink?

DINK WEBER: Sunlight is a good thing, but negative thinking can darken even the brightness of the sun. I believe the author is telling us that we need to rake the dead and dying leaves from our minds so we can see the happy colors again. We've got to get rid of stinkin' thinkin' and develop an attitude of gratitude.

RAY BARD: Any other favorite parts?

DINK WEBER: There's the quote from Willie Nelson at the beginning of chapter twelve: "Once you replace negative thoughts with positive ones, you'll start having positive results." And then there's the quote from Oliver Wendell Holmes at the beginning of chapter 16: "A mind once stretched by a new idea never regains its original dimension."

RAY BARD: Why those particular quotes?

DINK WEBER: With all due respect to the chaplain here, I don't see this as a religious story at all. You won't find a single instance in the entire story where the lawyer calls upon an invisible deity to save him from his troubles. Like I said earlier, it's about tenacity and perseverance. Believing in yourself. Not giving up. Overcoming adversity. We can do anything if we just keep positive. The only reference that might be considered even vaguely religious is the quote from the Native American medicine man at the end of chapter 29 that talks about how everything in the universe moves in circles. I say *Free the Beagle* is a story of human achievement. The only thing that would have made it better is if the lawyer had scratched his head once in a while and asked, "WWDWD."

CHAPLAIN CHANEY: What does that mean?

DINK WEBER: "What would Dink Weber do?" (general laughter around the room)

RAY BARD: So you're a humanist, then, Dink?

DINK WEBER: Absolutely. I believe that self-reliance is the key to successful living.

DR. DARCY DA SILVA: I'm sorry. What do you mean by the word "humanist"?

DINK WEBER: According to the American Humanist Association, "Humanism is a way of living, thinking, and acting that allows every individual to actualize his or her highest aspirations and successfully achieve a happy and fulfilling life. Humanists take responsibility for their own morals and their own lives, and for the lives of their communities and the world in which we live. Humanists emphasize reason and scientific inquiry, individual freedom and responsibility, human values and compassion, and the need for tolerance and cooperation. Humanists reject supernatural, authoritarian, and antidemocratic beliefs and doctrines."

CHAPLAIN CHANEY: In other words, humanists believe man is God.

TALYA MADORA: No, it sounds more to me like a humanist is a person who has Jewish beliefs without the Jewish faith.

DINK WEBER: Thank you, Talya. But the truth is that many humanists are religious people in a very conventional sense. There is Christian humanism, secular humanism, cultural humanism, philosophical humanism, and yes, there are many who see the true roots of humanism in the Torah. What all humanists have in common is a basic belief in the innate moral sense of humankind and the sanctity of the individual. The faith of a modern humanist, such as myself, is in the robustness of the human species, not necessarily in the protection and love of a supernatural being.

RAY BARD: But let's get back to the story. Chaplain, you were about to give us some other specific examples of why you're convinced the author is a Bible scholar?

CHAPLAIN CHANEY: Yes. The story begins when the lawyer glances at the newspaper, but doesn't really read it. Now, that newspaper contained good news for the lawyer, the gospel if you will, but the lawyer, like most of us today, was too busy dealing with all the cares of the day to sit down and actually read it. It stayed in his pocket throughout the whole journey. But if he had only taken the time to read it, he would have known that he was the Son of the King and that the beagle was a gift sent from Destinae, or heaven. Worst of all, at the end of chapter 10 we see the lawyer using the good news to spank his friend the beagle in much the same way that Christians beat each other up with the Bible every day. But just like the lawyer, they rarely take the time to read it and learn the truth about themselves and the value of the gifts that God has given them and the wonderful inheritance that awaits us at the end of our journey. And by the way, Dink, you forgot the second half of that quote from Willie Nelson. What he actually said was, "When I started counting my blessings, my whole life turned around."

RAY BARD: Anything else, Chaplain?

CHAPLAIN CHANEY: In the opening line of chapter 13, the lawyer has just partaken of the food that he desperately needs, and his first question is, "Does this hill have a name?" In the beagle story, the name of the hill is Epiphany, which means "a dazzling realization," but I believe the hill could just as easily be called Calvary or Golgotha.

RAY BARD: And your reasoning?

CHAPLAIN CHANEY: If you keep reading you'll see that after the hunter tells the lawyer the name of the hill, he immediately adds, "and not many can say to have climbed it." This is a clear echo of the words of Jesus in Matthew chapter 7, where he says, "the gate is small and the way is narrow that leads to life, and there are few who find it." And now that the lawyer has had this dazzling realization of the cross of Calvary, the very next sentence says, and I quote, "The beagle and I are going to Destinae." Obviously, Destinae is heaven, because no one ever returns from there. And then, in chapter 18, after the big storm has passed, it's Faith who is still standing on his rock. Now we're back in Matthew 7, where Jesus goes on to say, "Therefore everyone who hears these words of mine and puts them into practice is like a wise man who built his house on the rock. The rain came down, the streams rose, and the winds blew and beat against that house; yet it did not fall, because it had its foundation on the rock."

RAY BARD: So Pauline is seeing a rewrite of *The Wizard of Oz*, and Chaplain Chaney is seeing a rewrite of Matthew chapter 7, and Dink is seeing a nonreligious story of tenacity and perseverance, and Talya is seeing a guide to better business decisions. So where does the Sea of False Hope fit into all of this?

DINK WEBER: It's the place where all of society's ambitious parasites congregate.

TALYA MADORA: I thought it was just another sort of village of Compromise. Except that these were the white-collar people who didn't want to get their hands dirty.

DINK WEBER: It's society's leeches, I'm telling you. They're described in detail here in chapter 24. As a matter of fact, it goes so far as to name 'em. It says the lawyer saw "borrowers and bankers, gamblers and investors, ministers and politicians — each pacing intently back and forth, going nowhere." Now what was it that you were saying about the author's great love of religion, Chaplain?

CHAPLAIN CHANEY: Touché, Dink.

TALYA MADORA: Teacher, can I move? I don't think I want to sit between these two mean boys anymore.

RAY BARD: Talya, you've got your finger on something there in the manuscript. Is it something you wanted to point out to us?

TALYA MADORA: Yes. At the end of chapter 2, right after Judge Grey has given the lawyer his instructions and marched out of the room, it says the lawyer stood quietly and said to himself, "Surely an enemy has done this to me, but who? Who? Who?" And of course we later learn that there was never an enemy at all. The enemy existed only in the lawyer's mind.

DINK WEBER: Negative thinkin' again!

RAY BARD: Is this something you've experienced in business, Talya?

TALYA MADORA: Absolutely. When things are going badly, you always begin looking at your competitors as the source of your problems. But more often than not, the problem isn't outside your company, it's inside.

RAY BARD: Give us an example.

TALYA MADORA: You lose an important account to a competitor and you immediately assume they paid someone off to get the business, or told a lie about your product, or cheated in one of a hundred other ways. But the real reason you lost the business was probably inconsistent product quality, delays in shipping, a rude credit manager, or one of a thousand other little things that can cause a customer to begin to look elsewhere.

RAY BARD: What else have you got there?

TALYA MADORA: The end of chapter 5. It's dark outside and the lawyer has not been successful in his search for answers at the library. Judge Grey asks him, "Are you ready to begin your journey?" He replies, "I am here." That is, he doesn't directly answer the judge's question. And then the judge says, "All of us are counting on you, Counselor. We trust you won't let us down." Anyone who's ever been in charge knows that feeling extremely well.

RAY BARD: What feeling do you mean?

TALYA MADORA: It's the midnight hour. You can't put off your decision any longer. Everyone is counting on you. And you're not really sure what to do.

RAY BARD: Pauline, do you have anything you'd like to add to that?

PAULINE LEPINE: Only that I agree with Dr. da Silva. I've been absolutely fascinated with all these different interpretations.

RAY BARD: Dr. da Silva, are you ready to share your thoughts with us?

DR. DARCY DA SILVA: Yes. But first I would like to say that I have been deeply moved by the things the rest of you have seen in this story. Very little of this had occurred to me, and now I am anxious to go back to my room and read the story again, but more slowly this time.

RAY BARD: What did you see in the story, Dr. da Silva?

DR. DARCY DA SILVA: Whether or not the author is a modern humanist or a Bible scholar, I cannot say. But I can assure you that he knows something of the human brain.

RAY BARD: And what makes you say that, Doctor?

DR. DARCY DA SILVA: The story opens with seven quotes before the beginning of chapter one. In the first five of these, I felt that the author was trying to give us a strong sense of left-brain dominance, and indeed, we were about to witness exactly that in the lawyer. And then, in the comments found between chapters 1 and 2, the author actually goes into some detail in contrasting the functions of the left and right hemispheres of the brain. And then, in chapter 2, when I saw that Logic was the name of the judge who saw everything as black or white, I knew that the author was speaking of the left hemisphere. And the following sentence, "Judge Grey was another matter," made me absolutely certain.

RAY BARD: You say that it made you certain. So what did you think the story was about?

DR. DARCY DA SILVA: Grey matter. The brain. As a neurologist with a minor in psychology, I read the story as a beautiful allegory contrasting the intellectual functions of the left brain with the intuitive functions of the mute, right brain.

TALYA MADORA: Mute? Is that why you asked me what I meant by "dumb luck?"

DR. DARCY DA SILVA: Yes. All of the functions relating to human speech are found exclusively in the rules-and-duty-oriented, intellectual left hemisphere. The right brain, like the beagle, is dumb in that it cannot produce speech. But the right brain sees things that the left brain can never see.

RAY BARD: Elaborate on that a bit, please.

DR. DARCY DA SILVA: Do you remember when the lawyer and the beagle arrived at the cave of the avalanche on that first night, and the beagle immediately plunged inside, sniffing as she went, and then curled up and was soon fast asleep?

DINK WEBER: Yes.

DR. DARCY DA SILVA: And do you remember how the lawyer called her a "stupid beagle" and said "there could be a bear in that cave for all she knows?"

DINK WEBER: Yes.

DR. DARCY DA SILVA: So how did the beagle know that the cave was safe when the lawyer did not?

DINK WEBER: She was sniffing. She could smell it. The beagle had abilities the lawyer didn't have.

DR. DARCY DA SILVA: Yes. And in a very similar way, the intuitive right brain can sense many things that the intellectual left brain cannot detect. This is why the beagle is named Intuition, I believe.

RAY BARD: So you're really convinced that the book is about the brain, Dr. da Silva?

DR. DARCY DA SILVA: Oh yes, I am quite certain that it's about the brain. Most of the interchaptoral comments are contrasting the attributes of left-brain dominance with the attributes of right-brain dominance. The quotes from *The Odd Couple*, Lord Chesterfield, and Bruce Barton, and again from the movie about the gypsy woman. And then there are my personal favorites, the quotes from C-3PO about R2-D2.

RAY BARD: Why are those your favorites?

DR. DARCY DA SILVA: If you've seen the movie, you'll remember that C-3PO was very much like the lawyer and R2-D2 was like the beagle in that he could not speak, but was always plunging off into an adventure. Yes, there is no doubt that *Free the Beagle* was written about brain lateralization, but I now also believe that it was equally written about each of the things you've been discussing.

DINK WEBER: Is that really possible? Are you saying that Jim and I can both be right?

RAY BARD: Dink, I'm giving you and Jim one more shot at each other, but then you're going to have to kiss and make up.

DINK WEBER: I'll let Brother Chaney go first.

CHAPLAIN CHANEY: Okay, here's my parting salvo. Chapter 11 is called "The Terrible Truth," which is namely that all have sinned and fall short of the glory of God. Romans 3. Now keep in mind that in chapter 11 the lawyer is on the hilltop and the story tells us, and I'm quoting now, "Deep in his heart, the lawyer knew that he had failed and that he was about to die."

DINK WEBER: But he didn't die. The lawyer was just guilty of negative thinking, that's all.

CHAPLAIN CHANEY: Galatians 2, "I have been crucified with Christ and I no longer live, but Christ lives in me." Now, Dink, even you must have noticed the change in the lawyer after his hilltop experience?

DINK WEBER: Is it my turn now?

RAY BARD: Yes, Dink. Give us any final comments that you might have.

DINK WEBER: Is that recorder still on?

RAY BARD: Yes, it's still on.

DINK WEBER: And everything we say is going to be published?

RAY BARD: Fire away, Dink.

DINK WEBER: Well, I just wanted to say that I plan to add a whole new section to my own book, *The Power Within,* based on today's discussion, and that by the time these comments are published, the newly revised and expanded edition should be available online.

RAY BARD: Anything else, Dink?

DINK WEBER: Only that I'm delighted to have been invited.

RAY BARD: On behalf of the author, I want to thank each of you for participating. And for any of you who would like to meet the Wizard, he's waiting downstairs at the Bull and Bear to answer any questions you might have.

DR. DARCY DA SILVA: Very good.

TALYA MADORA: Excellent!

CHAPLAIN CHANEY: I was hoping to meet him.

DINK WEBER: Right now?

RAY BARD: Yes. Just past Bauman Rare Books is a stairway that leads down to the Bull and Bear.

TALYA MADORA: How will we recognize him?

RAY BARD: He's wearing an Irish cap made of all different colors of cloth patches.

TALYA MADORA: Like Joseph's coat.

DINK WEBER: With taste like that, I think I'm beginning to understand why you never put the Wizard's picture in his books, Ray!

RAY BARD: Goodbye, Dink. And thanks for coming.

DINK WEBER: Always remember, WWDWD!

RAY BARD: What would Dink Weber do.

DR. DARCY DA SILVA: Thank you for the invitation, Mr. Bard. It was good to meet you.

RAY BARD: And thank you for coming, Dr. da Silva. You made a very long trip to be here and we appreciate it tremendously.

DR. DARCY DA SILVA: I do have one more question.

RAY BARD: Yes?

DR. DARCY DA SILVA: Reading the story, I sensed the author had a hidden agenda in writing it. Can you tell me what he is hoping to accomplish?

RAY BARD: Balance, Dr. da Silva, only balance.

DR. DARCY DA SILVA: He hopes for the story to be used as an educational tool, then?

RAY BARD: You're very perceptive, doctor.

DR. DARCY DA SILVA: And he's wearing an Irish cap made of patches?

RAY BARD: Just down that way.

DR. DARCY DA SILVA: Thank you again.

TALYA MADORA: This was fun. I hope to see you again sometime.

RAY BARD: Thank you. And thank you for coming.

CHAPLAIN CHANEY: The book will be out in September?

RAY BARD: Yes, early September if everything stays on schedule.

CHAPLAIN CHANEY: Thanks for inviting me.

RAY BARD: And thank you for coming, Chaplain. We appreciated your comments.

CHAPLAIN CHANEY: We'll see you later, then.

RAY BARD: Goodbye.

PAULINE LEPINE: Well, evidently the public is less weary of the classic hero's journey than I originally thought. Those people were really taken with this little story!

RAY BARD: Pauline, every day I am amazed at the lessons that people see in it.

PAULINE LEPINE: Ray, if you don't mind, I'd like you to strike my comments. I just breezed through the book when I read it, and judging from what the others were saying, I think it might be worth a second read.

RAY BARD: I wish I could do that for you, Pauline, but the author was adamant that every word of today's discussion be transcribed exactly as spoken by the participants.

PAULINE LEPINE: Well, you can at least replace my name with a pseudonym, can't you?

RAY BARD: I can probably do that, as long as we don't change what was actually said.

PAULINE LEPINE: That would be great. Thanks.

RAY BARD: What name would you like me to use?

PAULINE LEPINE: How about John Leonard? Or Frank Kermode?

RAY BARD: No, really.

PAULINE LEPINE: Okay then, how about Pauline Lepine?

RAY BARD: There's not a critic by that name, is there?

PAULINE LEPINE: No.

RAY BARD: Okay, then. Pauline Lepine it is.

PAULINE LEPINE: Ray, tell me, how much has the author shared with you about this story, really?

RAY BARD: Do you mean how much of what you heard today was accurate interpretation and how much of it was just enthusiastic conjecture?

PAULINE LEPINE: Exactly.

RAY BARD: Well, the author told me before he ever began writing that the story would have a number of different interpretations, and that each one of them would be fully self-consistent. He said he was planning to write a literary Rubik's cube.

PAULINE LEPINE: You mean a story with six different faces?

RAY BARD: Something like that.

PAULINE LEPINE: So why were there were only five of us here today?

RAY BARD: I'm the sixth. My position was that it's simply an adventure story about a lawyer and a beagle on a journey. Remember?

PAULINE LEPINE: So you were the face-value interpretation.

RAY BARD: Yes.

PAULINE LEPINE: And what interpretation was I supposed to be?

RAY BARD: What do you mean?

PAULINE LEPINE: Obviously, I was supposed to see something that I failed to see.

RAY BARD: No, I think everything turned out exactly the way it was supposed to.

PAULINE LEPINE: Ray, I think that you know more than you're saying.

RAY BARD: All I can tell you is that the author drafted the invitation list himself and that he's a pretty amazing researcher.

PAULINE LEPINE: Has he ever shared with you any of the interpretations you heard today?

RAY BARD: Pauline, all together, the five of you brought forward less than ten percent of what he told me you might say. But I really can't say any more. Haven't you ever read any of his other books?

PAULINE LEPINE: Is that recorder still on?

RAY BARD: I agreed to leave it on until we had all left the room.

PAULINE LEPINE: Follow me.

RAY BARD: Really, Pauline, I can't say any more.

END OF TAPE

Have comments you want to share?
Want to read what others are saying about *Free the Beagle*?
Are you ready for the sequel?
Visit **www.FreeTheBeagle.com.**

Discussion Questions

Chapter 1 ~ Town Square

1. Why does the author give us the five quotations preceding chapter 1?

2. What might the shoeshine chair symbolize?

3. Does the "official clock" in the center of Town Square stand for anything? If so, what?

4. What might the newspaper stand represent?

5. When the lawyer sees the newspaper stand, he thinks to check the documents inside his briefcase. The shoeshine chair reminds him to check his shoes, and the clock reminds him to check his watch. But when he looks at the courthouse, he "[runs] his tongue smoothly across his teeth." Why?

6. When the lawyer feels "the familiar cold bulge ticking beneath his left vest pocket," what might this be besides his pocket watch?

7. Do you know anyone who acts like the lawyer does at the beginning of the story?

8. Do you ever think and act this way? If so, when?

9. We are told the lawyer "folded his crisp kerchief into six starched squares and placed it directly over his heart." Why six squares instead of eight? And why was the kerchief starched?

Chapter 2 ~ The Courthouse

10. Immediately before the beginning of chapter 2, the first mention of a dog follows a list contrasting the characteristics of the submissive right brain with those of the dominant left. In this list, can you spot any clues that might tell us why the author chose to make the lawyer masculine and the beagle feminine?

11. In the first paragraph, the characteristics of the courthouse are noted as "cold," "unyielding," and "hard," followed by "tomb," "click," and "fall." These are contrasted to the words "warm," "fuzzy," and "heart" in the same sentences. What does this say to you?

12. Judge Logic is "always dressed in perfect black and white." Why?

13. What is the final word of the sentence in which Judge Grey is first mentioned? Does this give us a clue to one of his several identities?

14. The lawyer is comfortable with Judge Logic, but uneasy around Judge Grey. Why?

15. When the judge answers the lawyer's question about "his cases," he answers over his shoulder. But when the lawyer asks about his journey, the judge turns to face him directly. Is this a clue to another alternate identity for Judge Grey? If so, who or what might he be?

16. Judge Grey denies the lawyer's request for "a schedule — charts, maps, a budget," and tells him, "Your journey will take what it takes." Think for a moment of all the journeys you will undertake in your life. What percentage do you think can be planned?

17. Standing quietly before the judge's bench, the lawyer is "staring into the distance" as he contemplates his fate, while the gallery shuffles toward the exits. Is the lawyer staring into space or time? Past or future? Reality or fantasy? And who or what is the gallery?

18. The unhappy lawyer thinks, "Surely an enemy has done this to me." Why does he immediately assume that his circumstances are the work of an enemy?

Chapter 3 ~ Poindexter

19. Prior to the beginning of chapter 3, we find a pair of quotes that can be read two ways. They can be interpreted to agree, or they can be interpreted to be mutually exclusive. Explain.

20. Immediately before chapter 3, why does the author choose to include this particular quote from *The Odd Couple*?

21. In the opening paragraph of chapter 3, we read that the lawyer "regained his sense of time and place." When and where did he lose his sense of time and place? And why?

22. In chapter 3, the lawyer feels the beagle as "a slight weight upon the tops of his feet." But in chapter 10, the beagle is "a slight weight upon his chest." Other than the fact that the lawyer is standing up in the first scene and lying on his back in the second, what might this difference symbolize?

23. Poindexter is the courthouse cat of Town Square. What else might Poindexter represent? (Your only other hint is in chapter 29.)

24. Poindexter bounces between the shoeshine chair and the newspaper stand before perching on top of the official clock in Town Square. Based on your earlier interpretation of the meanings of these three symbols, what is the meaning of this scene?

25. Other than the fact that she is a dog, why is it such a struggle for the beagle to climb up on the newspaper stand when it is obviously no trouble at all for Poindexter?

26. Who is Holly Golightly and what is the significance of this reference to her?

27. As the lawyer is taking the beagle home and the words on the collar's tag are echoing in his ears, we are pointedly told that Poindexter is "nowhere in sight." What is the significance of this?

Chapter 4 ~ The Library

28. We are told that no traveler has ever returned from Destinae. If this is one of its defining characteristics, what or where might Destinae be?

29. All those who write of Destinae speak of different ways to get there. Reconcile this with your answer to the question above.

30. In the light of your answers to questions 28 and 29, explain what is meant by "hacking through a jungle wilderness," "sailing uncharted seas," and "glittering parties and celebrities met along the way."

31. How many things in your own life might be called "Polaris"? Explain.

32. Who is the fool in chapter 4? Explain.

Chapter 5 ~ Has Anyone Seen Polaris?

33. In the lawyer's briefcase are "his diploma from Law School, a copy of every possible chart and map . . . and all the money that he could gather." Please explain the significance of each as they relate to the lawyer's perception of what lies ahead.

34. The first appearance of Polaris is in the sky "beyond the official clock." How might this be interpreted? Explain.

35. After gaining the lawyer's attention, the beagle appears to look for someone before turning to fix her gaze firmly on the lawyer. What is the significance of this? Explain how it relates to what happens next.

36. The farmer who points out Polaris speaks with a distinctive accent but is given no name. How many other people do we later meet in the story who fit this description? Is this significant?

37. After the farmer speaks, he looks at the beagle and she wags her tail. Why? Does this tell us anything about the farmer? About the beagle?

38. Name two of the things that Judge Grey might have meant when he said, "All of us are counting on you, Counselor. We trust you won't let us down"?

39. Other than the fact that it's another word for "lawyer," what is the significance of the appellation "Counselor" in this story?

40. Have you ever "walked off into the darkness," guided only by an unreachable "gleam in the sky"? Explain.

Chapter 6 ~ Marching by Moonlight

41. Prior to chapter 6, we read the first of many quotes from C-3PO. Assuming that the author is comparing C-3PO and R2-D2 to the lawyer and the beagle, which is which? Explain your reasoning.

42. Why does the lawyer consider the beagle to be stupid? Is the beagle stupid? Explain.

43. When the lawyer "spread his kerchief on the cleanest patch of ground he could find," what kind of ground might this have been? Explain.

44. In the candlelight, "the cave walls [dance] with magical patterns," but the lawyer doesn't seem to notice. Is this significant? Explain.

45. The lawyer places a heavy rock on the leash of the beagle in order to restrain her. Is his attempt successful? Is there a symbolic significance in this action? Explain.

Chapter 7 ~ BOOM!

46. Before chapter 7, we read a quote from *The Wizard of Oz* in which the Wicked Witch of the West says, "I'll get you, my pretty! And your little dog, too!" If the Wicked Witch is a symbol of a person or a force in the life of the lawyer, who or what might she be?

47. The beagle becomes anxious long before the lawyer. How might she have known of the impending landslide?

48. What might be symbolized by the heavy rock the lawyer lays on the leash of the beagle?

49. Other than the fact that the cave has been covered by a landslide, what is meant by the sentence, "The cave where the lawyer had been sleeping moments ago was now sealed off from sunlight forever"? What sunlight might this be?

50. Only moments earlier, the lawyer had been furious that the beagle had made him leave the dryness of the cave. Following the avalanche, "the lawyer was very happy to be standing in the rain." Have you ever experienced a quick reversal like this? Explain.

Chapter 8 ~ In the Belly of Confusion

51. When the lawyer gets his first glimpse of the endless Forest of Confusion, he pauses and swallows before going on. Have you ever felt overwhelmed or daunted? Explain.

52. After the lawyer has entered the forest, we read, "Sunlight doesn't look like sunlight when it's filtered through dead and dying leaves. And along the edges of their shadows you will find no happy colors." Other than describing the sunlight, do these sentences have another meaning? If so, what might it be?

53. When the beagle senses an intruder hiding behind a tree on the other side of the lawyer, she growls and "[stretches] her leash tightly in his direction." The lawyer misinterprets and spanks her for it. Have you ever misinterpreted your own intuition? Explain.

54. Worry is described as "a shadowy gentleman in a formal riding coat." Is worry like this? Explain.

55. When Worry says, "I'm here to help you," might he possibly be sincere? Explain.

56. Worry claims to have been born in the Forest of Confusion. Do you believe his claim? Explain.

57. The beagle is never comfortable with Worry. Why not?

Chapter 9 ~ "Please allow me to introduce myself..."

58. When Worry says, "Keep a tight hold on that beagle, kind sir," he's only telling the lawyer to continue doing what the lawyer has done since the beginning of the story. Does the lawyer share any other characteristics with Worry? If so, explain.

59. Have you ever leashed your beagle when you should have let her run free? Explain.

60. Worry has a benign veneer, but Fear is obviously a thug. Explain.

61. When the lawyer is overtaken by Panic and loses control of his senses, Fear smiles "an ugly, bad-teeth smile." What are the teeth of Fear?

62. Panic is referred to as Fear's "heavier, twitching twin" and we're told that he thumps "a stick into his open palm, rat-a-tat-tat." Why would Panic be heavier and twitching? And why would the beat he taps be staccato?

63. Name at least two things the author might have meant when he wrote that "Fear and Panic were thirstily absorbed into the soft edges of darkness."

Chapter 10 ~ Nameless and Homeless

64. What might the author be trying to imply by placing the *Calvin and Hobbes* quote immediately after chapter 9?

65. Why does the beagle chew through her leash?

66. The lawyer uses his belt to bind the beagle. What might the lawyer's belt symbolize?

67. Like the lawyer's belt, the newspaper that the lawyer uses to spank the beagle is symbolic of something. What might this be?

68. Other than the fact that it contains only four pages, why does the author specifically describe the newspaper as "thin"?

69. If we believe that no words in the story are used frivolously, what might it mean when we are told that the lawyer instinctively places the refolded newspaper "in the bottom left pocket of his jacket"? Has this location been specified for a reason? If so, how might it be symbolically significant?

70. Now without a belt, the lawyer's "pants dropped occasionally and exposed his bare bottom to the world. And the leaves of the forest laughed quietly every time it happened." What might the author be trying to say here?

Chapter 11 ~ The Terrible Truth

71. Based on the clue given to us in the *Star Wars* quote that immediately precedes chapter 11, what might we surmise about the lawyer's feelings toward the beagle? Explain.

72. In the Forest of Confusion, the lawyer finds it "difficult to discern daylight from darkness." Other than the effects of a forest canopy, what might this passage describe?

73. While hopelessly lost in the Forest of Confusion, the lawyer feels the nights "growing steadily colder." What might these cold nights represent? Have you ever experienced a time like this in your own life? Explain.

74. The lawyer and the beagle experience a desperate need for food while in the Forest of Confusion. Other than bodily sustenance, what might this "food" be? Explain.

75. Dangerously lost in the Swamp of Depression, the lawyer "allowed the slight incline to guide his footsteps in the darkness. If a step seemed easy, he knew it was leading him downward. It was only the more difficult steps that would take him higher." Is it usually the difficult steps that take us higher in life? Can you name some of the "easy" steps that take us downward?

76. When the lawyer makes it to the top of the hill, he sees a "forest that seemed to have no end. And no way out." Have you ever felt this way? Explain.

77. The lawyer has a plan to reach Destinae, but when that plan seems hopelessly unattainable, he falls into despair and says, "Destinae does not exist." He has no idea that the most important moment in his journey is about to happen. Have you ever been at the end of your strength when your answer finally came? Explain.

78. When the lawyer has freed the beagle and believes he is about to die, he remembers the clock in Town Square and whispers, "I wonder what time it is now." Explain.

Chapter 12 ~ Consolation

79. Following chapter 11, we read quotes from Willie Nelson and C-3PO. Why do you think these particular quotes were chosen to appear precisely here?

80. When the lawyer has resigned himself to his dark fate, he thinks of the newspaper stand and laughs. Then he looks at his shoes and laughs harder still. Why?

81. The hunter has an accent much like the farmer who revealed Polaris to the lawyer. Is this a coincidence, or is it somehow meaningful? Explain.

82. We are never told the name of the hunter. What name would you give him?

83. Of all the breeds of dogs, why do you suppose the author chose to write about the beagle?

Chapter 13 ~ The Ship Dock a'Luff

84. "Epiphany is the name o' this hill," says the hunter, "and na' many can say to'a' climbed it." Considering the name of the hill, why are we not surprised that not many can say to have climbed it?

85. If the hunter had no accent, how might he have pronounced "the ship dock a'Luff"?

86. After the lawyer's fireside chat with the hunter, we read, "When the lawyer awakened, [1] the fire was out, [2] the hunter was gone, and [3] the beagle was staring northward." Please elaborate on what each of these three things might mean.

Chapter 14 ~ Winter Cave of Introspection

87. No less than four interchaptoral comments are found between chapters 13 and 14. Please explain why the author chose to insert each of these precisely here.

88. Does it make sense that the Cave of Introspection would be located in the side of the Hill of Epiphany? Explain.

89. Running free and unfettered, the beagle becomes stronger during the winter. And to her, the Forest of Confusion is "a Forest of Opportunity." Why is it so easy for the beagle when it has been so hard for the lawyer? Explain.

90. In his final conversation with the lawyer at Epiphany, the hunter refuses to accept the lawyer's gold watch and claims "the time for me is always now an' now is a time that ne'er changes." What might the hunter mean by this statement? Does it give you any clue to his identity? Explain.

91. When the beagle's nose touches the lawyer's nose, the lawyer has a sudden realization. Of what might the beagle's nose be symbolic?

Chapter 15 ~ Children of the Ship Dock

92.   The lawyer and the beagle spend the winter in the Cave of Introspection. Explain how introspection is like a cave.

93.   Looking back at the interchaptoral comments preceding chapter 2, does it make sense for the male puppy to be named Faith and the female puppy to be named Hope? Explain.

94.   "And when the thawing winds of spring arrived, the snow and ice were completely melted." To what snow and ice does this refer?

95.   What does the author imply through his selection of quotes at the end of chapter 15 and beginning of chapter 16?

Chapter 16 ~ Spring Storm

96.   Why is Intuition able to lead the way "north by north" when the lawyer has not been able?

97.   "The wind sang sweetly [and] the forest blew away like fog." Then, "singing winds became stinging winds" as a storm ambushed the lawyer and the beagles. Have you ever begun a happy day that abruptly took a turn for the worse? Explain.

98.   As soon as the storm begins, Faith crawls out of the ditch and onto a rock to "[bark] defiance at the storm." Is this rock an important symbol? Explain.

Chapter 17 ~ Rain

99.   During the storm, Hope is obedient while Faith is defiant. Is this typical of the difference between Faith and Hope? Explain.

100. The lawyer and the beagle find it difficult to communicate with each other during the storm. Are most "storms" in your own life like this? Explain.

Chapter 18 ~ The River of Hate

101. When the storm is over, "a trembling lawyer and a muddy beagle [rise] shakily from the ground to survey the pointless

scene." The word "pointless" seems to imply that not everything happens for a reason. What is your opinion? Is everything that happens meant to happen, or do some things happen for no reason? Explain.

102. The River of Hate is described as shallow, dirty, and cold. Explain.

103. We are told very specifically that the River of Hate "did not flow to the north." Why is this important?

104. We are told that the lawyer "shouted to no one." Have you ever done this? Why?

105. As he follows the River of Hate, the lawyer trips and falls on a stone. What might this stone represent?

Chapter 19 ~ Village of Compromise

106. As they continue along the River of Hate, the trio travel "under spacious skies staring directly into the sun." Is the reference to spacious skies important here? Explain.

107. Of what might the sun be a symbol? Explain.

108. The Village of Compromise first appears when the lawyer is in despair. Is this significant? Explain.

109. We are told that the doors on the houses of Compromise are "exactly in the middle." Why might this be so?

110. The people of Compromise seem proud of their humility. Have you ever known anyone like this? Explain.

111. Bread and beer are easily had in Compromise, and no one seems anxious to leave. Of what might this bread and beer be symbolic? Explain.

112. The people of Compromise seem to believe that they should be "content with such things as nature has chosen to give." Are such people more likely, or less likely, to believe that "everything happens for a reason"? Explain.

113. Explain how the Alfred de Musset quote at the beginning of chapter 19 relates to the story.

Chapter 20 ~ Contentment in the Village

114. The lawyer has become comfortable in Compromise when he learns that the villagers are offended by any discussion of fruit: "And we do not bear much fruit in Compromise." Explain all that you believe might be meant by this statement.

115. When the lawyer chooses "to press the matter further," he begins to act like an attorney who is digging for the truth. Does his inquisitive nature and demand for detail serve him well in this instance? Explain.

Chapter 21 ~ "Aroo! Aroo-aroo!"

116. As the mayor is beginning to explain to the lawyer how he came to arrive in Compromise, he acts "as though he were about to bestow great wisdom upon the lawyer." Have you ever known anyone like this?

117. Explain the lawyer's final statement to the mayor: "You should have had a beagle!"

118. It is only after the lawyer is reunited with Hope that he dreams "great and colorful dreams with three smelly dogs. . . ." How do you interpret this statement?

Chapter 22 ~ Climbing the Purple Mountains

119. As the lawyer climbs the Purple Mountains, he realizes that Hope has never been in Compromise, but immediately continued following Polaris after she recovered from the storm. What does this say about the lawyer's decision to search for Hope by following the River of Hate?

120. Sitting upon the crest of the Purple Mountains and with a sympathetic tear falling off his chin, the lawyer laments that the people of Compromise "don't even know what they're missing." To what do you think he is referring?

121. In your opinion, why does the beagle bark at Compromise from the crest of the Purple Mountains?

Chapter 23 ~ Across the Fruited Plain

122. What does the wide variety of fruits available on the Fruited Plain tell us about the place?

123. Why does the lawyer immediately believe the city along the shore to be Destinae?

124. What is a commiphora tree? What is harvested from it? Why might the author have chosen to include such a tree in his description of the fruited plain?

125. Spotting Polaris from the Fruited Plain, the lawyer begins to change his theory about the location of Destinae. Why?

Chapter 24 ~ Ocean of Tears

126. How does the Thomas Pynchon quote at the beginning of chapter 24 relate to the lawyer's new conclusion about the location of Destinae? How does it relate to the ambitions of the people in chapter 24?

127. On the proud and majestic ship dock is a wide variety of people "pacing intently back and forth, going nowhere." They are just "waiting for their ship to come in." Do you know anyone like this? Explain.

128. What do people really mean when they say they're "waiting for their ship to come in"? Explain.

129. People in the City by the Sea want to know if the lawyer has "connections" or knows "the name of a good agent." What might this tell us about them?

130. The people on the ship dock tell exciting stories about the ships they believe will come and take them away in splendor to Destinae. Why do you suppose the lawyer accepts these stories at face value?

Chapter 25 ~ A Ticket to Ride

131. As the lawyer speaks to the people who are waiting for their ship to come in, a man tells him that one has to have "the right combination" to win. What might the man mean by this? Explain.

132. One of the women on the ship dock tells the lawyer, "Good things come to those who wait." Have you found this to be true in you own life? Explain.

Chapter 26 ~ The Leap of Faith

133. After Faith and Intuition leap off the ship dock, the lawyer assumes that Intuition will quickly catch up to Faith and bring him back unharmed, so he is more than a little alarmed when he sees Intuition take the lead and continue swimming northward. Have you ever been surprised like this? Explain.

134. As the lawyer continues his journey with new determination, he holds Hope above him as he bounces along the bottom. Explain why he might have done this.

135. Why is it appropriate that Faith leads the way across the Sea of False Hope? Explain.

Chapter 27 ~ Knee Deep

136. The water in the Sea of False Hope isn't drinkable. What might this signify?

Chapter 28 ~ Diamonds of a Princess

137. Why might the author have chosen to compare the glitter on the water of the Sea of False Hope to the diamonds in the necklace of a princess? Explain.

138. "But the water was getting neither shallower nor deeper. . . . The lawyer's hips ached from their constant struggle against it, and he wished with all his heart that he could lie down." Have you ever felt this way? Explain.

139. We are told that Hope was never allowed to lead because "no one quite trusted her sense of direction." Have you ever failed to trust hope in your own life? How is this different from faith? Explain.

Chapter 29 ~ Destinae!

140. When the travelers reach Destinae, what do you feel is the energy that forms "a mighty fountain of light spraying up and out in every direction without ever making a sound"?

141. Why do you think the lawyer feels the park bench to be "strangely familiar" and "somehow out of place"? Explain.

Chapter 30 ~ Town Without a Square

142. According to your own interpretation of the story, what does it mean when we read, "The lawyer and the beagles awoke to the beginning of a brand new day"? Explain.

143. According to your own interpretation of the story, who or what are the "soldiers without uniforms, books without covers, buildings without ceilings or walls" in the city of Destinae?

144. According to your own interpretation of the story, what is implied when we read, "And instead of a ticking, official clock, Destinae has a fountain at its heart"?

Chapter 31 ~ End of the Line

145. "It was the proudest moment of his life. And the most cruel." Can proud moments also be cruel? Explain.

146. According to your own interpretation of the story, what is implied when you read that the lawyer "quickly chose a road leading out of town and hurried down it — with all three beagles"?

Chapter 32 ~ Taking the Road Not Taken

147. Outside the town, the lawyer sits "in a field freshly wounded by the ripping steel of a plow." Why is this an appropriate place for the lawyer to sit?

148. Who, in your opinion, is the farmer who speaks to the lawyer about seed? What name would you give him?

Chapter 33 ~ Meeting the Son of the King

149. Upon his arrival in Destinae, the lawyer believes himself to be the messenger, and the beagle to be a gift to someone else. Have you ever been guilty of the lawyer's mistake? Explain.

150. Why might the King have wanted his son to endure the hardships of the journey before he inherited the kingdom? Explain.

In Search of the Beagle

151. In the roundtable discussion that followed the story, which of the participants did you most identify with? Why?

Bonus Question

152. Few things, if any, are accidental in this book. So why are there 33 chapters?

About Wizard Academy

"Alice in Wonderland on steroids! I wish Roy Williams had been my very first college professor. If he had been, everything I learned after that would have made a lot more sense and been a lot more useful. . . . Astounding stuff."
   DR. LARRY MCCLEARY
   NEUROLOGIST AND THEORETICAL PHYSICIST

"Be prepared to take a wild, three-ring-circus journey into the creative recesses of the brain. For anyone who must think critically or write creatively on the job, the Wizard Academy is a must."
   DR. KEVIN RYAN, PRESIDENT
   THE EXECUTIVE WRITER

"Valuable, helpful, insightful, and thought provoking. We're recommending it to everyone we see."
   JAN NATIONS AND STERLING TARRANT, SENIOR MANAGERS
   FOCUS ON THE FAMILY

"Even with all I knew, I was not fully prepared for the experience I had at the Academy. . . . Who else but a wizard can make sense of so many divergent ideas? I highly recommend it."
   MARK HUFFMAN, ADVERTISING PRODUCTION MANAGER
   PROCTER & GAMBLE

"A life-altering 72 hours."
   JIM RUBART